LEISURE ARTS' BEST
TeddyBear
·T·R·E·A·S·U·R·Y·

LEISURE ARTS, INC.

and

OXMOOR HOUSE, INC.

TeddyBear
·TREASURY·

Teddy bears are a symbol of the innocence of childhood, the comfort of family and friends, and our own capacity to love. With their wholesome charm, it's easy to see why our furry little friends have been cherished ever since the early 1900's, when they were named after President Theodore "Teddy" Roosevelt. Our must-have Treasury of Teddy Bears contains an abundance of irresistible scenes that remind us of our childhood buddy's talent for sharing a belly laugh or offering a snuggly bear hug. This versatile collection includes sweatshirts and samplers, afghans and aprons, towels and totes, and more, in a volume brimming over with ideas for home decorating, clothing, and gifts. Like peanut butter and jelly, teddy bears and cross stitch are such perfect partners that you'll "bearly" be able to put down this book!

EDITORIAL STAFF

Vice President and Editor-in-Chief:
Anne Van Wagner Childs
Executive Director: Sandra Graham Case
Editorial Director: Susan Frantz Wiles
Publications Director: Carla Bentley
Creative Art Director: Gloria Bearden
Senior Graphics Art Director: Melinda Stout

EDITORIAL
Managing Editor: Linda L. Trimble
Associate Editors: Darla Burdette Kelsay and
Janice Teipen Wojcik
Assistant Editors: Tammi Williamson Bradley,
Terri Leming Davidson, and Karen Walker
Copy Editor: Laura Lee Weland

TECHNICAL
Senior Publications Editor: Sherry Taylor O'Connor
Special Projects Editor: Connie White Irby
Senior Production Assistant: Martha H. Carle

ART
Book/Magazine Graphics Art Director:
Diane M. Hugo
Senior Production Graphics Illustrator: Guniz Jernigan
Production Graphics Illustrator: Bridgett Shrum

BUSINESS STAFF

Publisher: Bruce Akin
Vice President, Marketing: Guy A. Crossley
Vice President and General Manager: Thomas L. Carlisle
Retail Sales Director: Richard Tignor
Vice President, Retail Marketing: Pam Stebbins
Retail Marketing Director: Margaret Sweetin
Retail Customer Services Manager: Carolyn Pruss
General Merchandise Manager: Russ Barnett
Vice President, Finance: Tom Siebenmorgen
Distribution Director: Ed M. Strackbein

Library of Congress Catalog Number 97-73652
Hardcover ISBN 0-8487-4165-X
Softcover ISBN 1-57486-077-1

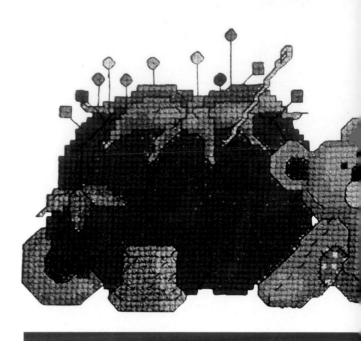

Table of Contents

Teddy Bear Reunion

When relatives or longtime friends gather for a visit, their reunion is bound to rekindle fond memories and inspire lots of love and laughter. The heartwarming scenes in this collection recall such tender moments. With open arms and friendly smiles, the extended teddy bear family in our Bear Family Welcome will lend a touch of warmth and hospitality to your home and remind you of your own beloved kinfolk.

"...nily and Me Welcome Jhee"

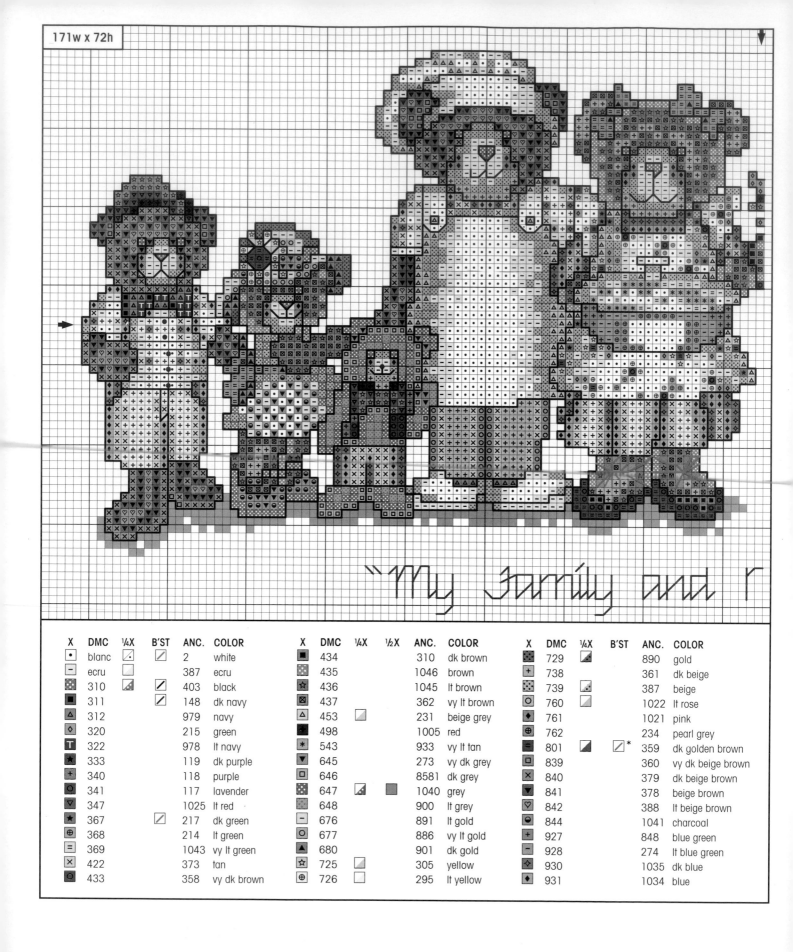

171w x 72h

"My Family and r

X	DMC	¼X	B'ST	ANC.	COLOR	X	DMC	¼X	½X	ANC.	COLOR	X	DMC	¼X	B'ST	ANC.	COLOR
•	blanc	◪	◿	2	white	◼	434			310	dk brown	▨	729	◿		890	gold
−	ecru	◻		387	ecru	▨	435			1046	brown	+	738			361	dk beige
▩	310	◪	◿	403	black	☆	436			1045	lt brown	▨	739	◿		387	beige
◼	311		◿	148	dk navy	⊠	437			362	vy lt brown	○	760	◿		1022	lt rose
▲	312			979	navy	△	453	◻		231	beige grey	◆	761			1021	pink
◇	320			215	green	◼	498			1005	red	⊕	762			234	pearl grey
T	322			978	lt navy	✳	543			933	vy lt tan	▤	801	◪	◿*	359	dk golden brown
★	333			119	dk purple	▼	645			273	vy dk grey	▭	839			360	vy dk beige brown
+	340			118	purple	▢	646			8581	dk grey	⊠	840			379	dk beige brown
○	341			117	lavender	▨	647	◪	◼	1040	grey	▼	841			378	beige brown
▽	347			1025	lt red	▢	648			900	lt grey	♡	842			388	lt beige brown
★	367		◿	217	dk green	−	676			891	lt gold	⊖	844			1041	charcoal
⊕	368			214	lt green	○	677			886	vy lt gold	+	927			848	blue green
=	369			1043	vy lt green	▲	680			901	dk gold	−	928			274	lt blue green
✕	422			373	tan	☆	725	◻		305	yellow	✧	930			1035	dk blue
◎	433			358	vy dk brown	⊕	726	◻		295	lt yellow	◆	931			1034	blue

8

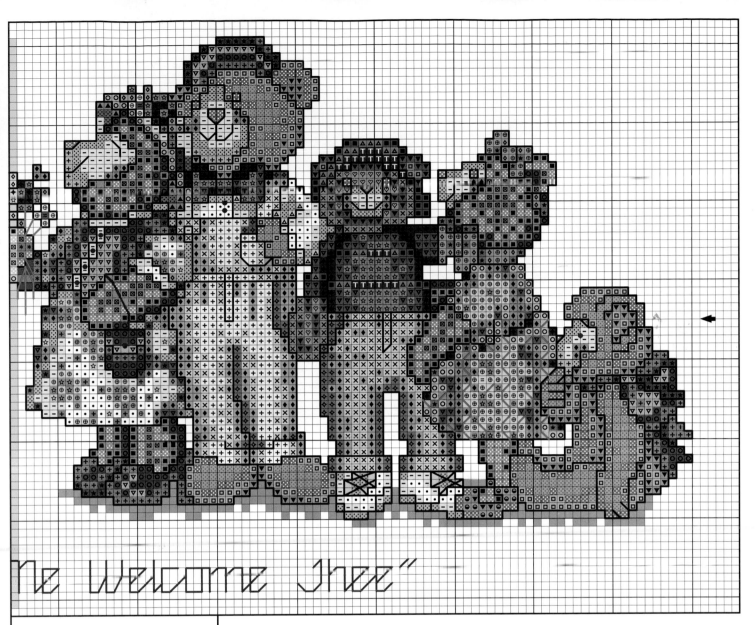

"We Welcome Thee"

X	DMC	¼X	ANC.	COLOR
×	932		1033	lt blue
	3072		847	vy lt grey
☆	3328		1024	rose
⊕	3713		1020	lt pink
▽	3747		120	lt lavender
+	3752		1032	vy lt blue
=	3821			dk yellow
O	3828			dk tan
•	310			black French Knot
	Blue area indicates last row of left section of design.			
*	Use 2 strands of floss.			

The design was stitched over 2 fabric threads on a 22" x 14" piece of Antique White Lugana (25 ct). Three strands of floss were used for Cross Stitch, 1 strand for Backstitch and Half Cross Stitch, and 2 strands for French Knots, unless otherwise noted in the color key. It was custom framed.

Design by Darcy Gerdes.
Needlework adaptation by Jane Chandler.

CHATTER HAT BEARS

Donning their Sunday bonnets, this trio of beribboned bears gathers to pass an afternoon chatting about the latest fashion trends.

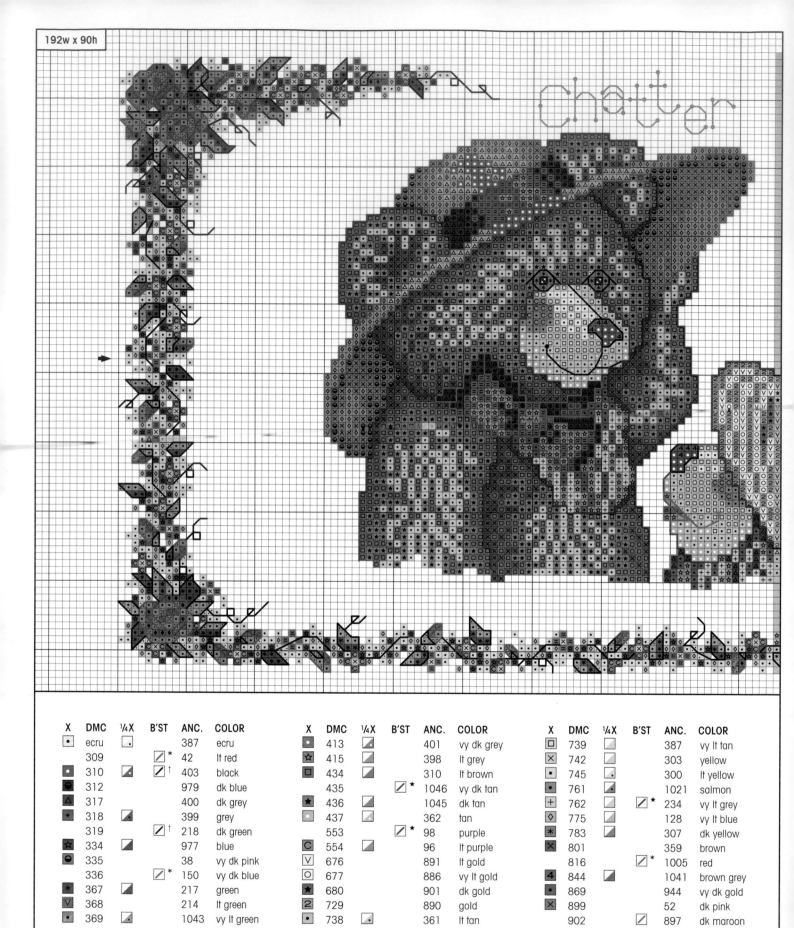

192w x 90h

X	DMC	¼X	B'ST	ANC.	COLOR	X	DMC	¼X	B'ST	ANC.	COLOR	X	DMC	¼X	B'ST	ANC.	COLOR
•	ecru	•		387	ecru	•	413	◿		401	vy dk grey	▢	739	◿		387	vy lt tan
	309		◿ *	42	lt red	☆	415	◿		398	lt grey	✕	742	◿		303	yellow
■	310	◿	◿ †	403	black	▢	434	◿		310	lt brown	•	745	•		300	lt yellow
⬤	312			979	dk blue		435		◿ ★	1046	vy dk tan	•	761	◿		1021	salmon
△	317			400	dk grey	★	436			1045	dk tan	+	762		◿ *	234	vy lt grey
•	318	◿		399	grey	▣	437	◿		362	tan	◇	775			128	vy lt blue
	319		◿ †	218	dk green		553		◿ ★	98	purple	✳	783			307	dk yellow
☆	334	◿		977	blue	C	554	◿		96	lt purple	✕	801			359	brown
◉	335			38	vy dk pink	V	676			891	lt gold		816		◿ *	1005	red
	336		◿ *	150	vy dk blue	O	677			886	vy lt gold	4	844	◿		1041	brown grey
✳	367	◿		217	green	★	680			901	dk gold	•	869			944	vy dk gold
V	368			214	lt green	2	729			890	gold	✕	899			52	dk pink
•	369	◿		1043	vy lt green	•	738	◿		361	lt tan		902		◿	897	dk maroon

12

X	DMC	¼X	B'ST	ANC.	COLOR
◉	915	☑ ♦		1029	dk mauve
⊟	917	◨		89	mauve
	938		☑	381	dk brown
◇	962			75	pink
▣	963			73	vy lt pink
V	3325			129	lt blue
☆	3607	◨		87	lt mauve
▲	3685			1028	maroon
◆	3712	◨		1023	dk salmon
C	3713			1020	lt salmon
◮	3716			25	lt pink
	3799	☑ ♦		236	steel grey
◉	310				black French Knot

X	DMC	
⊙	902	dk maroon French Knot
◉	915	dk mauve French Knot
▣		Blue area indicates first row of right section of design.
*		Use vy dk blue for center hat ribbon, red for roses, and lt red for all other.
†		Use black for facial features and dk green for all other.
✶		Use purple for flowers, vy lt grey for highlights in eyes, and vy dk tan for all other.
♦		Use dk mauve for letters and flowers and steel grey for all other.

The design was stitched over 2 fabric threads on a 24" x 16" piece of Cream Lugana (25 ct). Three strands of floss were used for Cross Stitch, 2 strands for Backstitch and French Knots in letters, and 1 strand for all other Backstitch and French Knots. It was custom framed.

Design by Darcy Gerdes.
Needlework adaptation by Jane Chandler.

Assembled for a family portrait, these country cousins will steal your heart! The cuddly clan offers a charming border for our afghan, which is sure to delight a "beary" special someone.

X	DMC	¼X	B'ST	ANC.	COLOR	X	DMC	¼X	B'ST	ANC.	COLOR
•	blanc			2	white	−	739			387	cream
◧	310	◢	✓	403	black	•	822			390	lt beige
◼	347		✓	1025	red	▲	838			380	vy dk brown
★	433			358	vy dk tan	★	839			360	dk brown
◉	434			310	dk tan	−	840			379	brown
V	435			1046	tan	+	841			378	lt brown
•	436			1045	lt tan	−	930		✓	1035	blue
✳	610			889	vy dk khaki	◇	932		✓	1033	lt blue
◻	611			898	dk khaki	☆	3072			847	vy lt grey
+	612			832	khaki	✕	3712		✓	1023	lt red
4	613			831	lt khaki	5	3790			393	vy dk beige
◻	642			392	dk beige	•	310		black French Knot		
2	644			830	beige		Grey area indicates first row of bottom section				
◉	646			8581	dk grey		of design.				
+	647			1040	grey		Blue lines indicate raised border of				
•	648			900	lt grey		stitching area.				
☆	738			361	vy lt tan						

The designs were stitched over 2 fabric threads on a 45" x 58" piece (standard afghan size) of Ivory Abby Cloth (18 ct).

Referring to Diagram for placement of designs on afghan, center and stitch **Design #1** in corner stitching areas. Center **Design #2** in stitching area of each short end (**Design #2** fits exactly in stitching area of short end). Six strands of floss were used for Cross Stitch, 2 strands for black Backstitch and French Knots, and 3 strands for all other Backstitch.

For afghan, cut selvages from fabric; measure 5½" from raw edge of fabric and pull out one fabric thread. Fringe fabric up to missing thread. Repeat for each side. Tie an overhand knot at each corner with 4 horizontal and 4 vertical fabric threads. Working from corners, use 8 fabric threads for each knot until all threads are knotted.

Designs by Jane Chandler.

Some of our fondest childhood memories are of the fun times spent hanging out with our best friends. Whether you stitch this cute design to resemble a snapshot or use only a portion of it on a cozy afghan, these true-blue bear buddies will remind you of your own playful pals.

17

177w x 90h

X	DMC	¼X	B'ST	ANC.	COLOR	X	DMC	¼X	B'ST	ANC.	COLOR	X	DMC	¼X	½X	ANC.	COLOR
•	blanc			2	white		550			102	purple		798			131	lt royal blue
=	ecru			387	ecru		552			99	lt purple		813			161	lt blue
•	310			403	black	P	611			898	dk khaki		815			43	dk red
▲	318			399	grey blue		612			832	khaki		825			162	dk blue
	321			9046	red		646			8581	dk grey		826			161	blue
	413			401	vy dk grey blue		648			900	grey	H	827			160	vy lt blue
	414			235	dk grey blue		666			46	lt red	▲	838			380	vy dk beige brown
	415			398	lt grey blue		726			295	yellow		839			360	dk beige brown
V	433			358	brown	+	727			293	lt yellow		840			379	beige brown
	434			310	lt brown		738			361	lt tan	V	841			378	lt beige brown
	435			1046	vy dk tan	•	739			387	vy lt tan		842			388	vy lt beige brown
	436			1045	dk tan		762			234	vy lt grey blue		844			1041	vy dk grey
	437			362	tan		797			132	royal blue		898			360	dk brown

X	DMC	1/4X	B'ST	ANC.	COLOR
■	910	◪		229	dk green
∙	911			205	green
+	912			209	lt green
■	915	◪	*	1029	dk violet
■	917			89	violet
4	924			851	vy dk blue grey
◉	926			850	blue grey
❖	927			848	lt blue grey
■	938	◪		381	vy dk brown
=	954			203	vy lt green
◆	986			246	vy dk green
✕	3033			391	lt beige
+	3072			847	lt grey

X	DMC	ANC.	COLOR
Σ	3607	87	lt violet
∙	3768	779	dk blue grey
△	3782	899	beige
◉	blanc		white French Knot
●†	310		black French Knot
▨			Pink area indicates first row of right section of design.

* For afghan, use 4 strands. For framed piece, use 3 strands.

† For framed piece, use 2 strands.

The entire design was stitched over 2 fabric threads on a 23" x 16" piece of Cream Lugana (25 ct). Three strands of floss were used for Cross Stitch and 1 strand for Half Cross Stitch, Backstitch, and French Knots, unless otherwise noted in the color key. It was custom framed.

The bears only (refer to photo) were stitched over 2 fabric threads on a 45" x 58" piece (standard afghan size) of Soft White Anne Cloth (18 ct). Six strands of floss were used for Cross Stitch and 2 strands for Backstitch, and French Knots, unless otherwise noted in the color key. For afghan finishing and design placement, see Afghan Finishing, page 143.

Design by Darcy Gerdes.
Needlework adaptation by Jane Chandler.

19

TEDDY'S
TEA PARTY

When little girls throw a tea party, teddy bears are often the guests of honor. Dressed in their finery, these sophisticated friends sip cups of imaginary tea and dream of becoming young ladies. The sweet portrait is sure to delight any little miss.

X	DMC	¼X	½X	B'ST	ANC.	COLOR
•	blanc	⦚		⦚	2	white
▬	311				148	dk blue
Π	334				977	blue
d	353	◪			6	peach
▬	433	◪			358	dk brown
	434			⦚	310	brown
%	435	◪			1046	lt brown
⊠	436	◪			1045	dk tan
⬟	437	◪			362	tan
	500		▨		683	dk green
⬜	501		▨		878	green
	503		▨		876	lt green
	640			⦚	903	dk beige
P	644				830	beige
O	712				926	cream
●	738	◪			361	lt tan
V	739	◪			387	vy lt tan
8	754	◪			1012	lt peach
◉	758	◪			882	lt flesh
✕	760				1022	rose
C	761	◪			1021	lt rose
=	775	◪			128	lt grey blue
△	819				271	lt pink
2	822	◻			390	lt beige
P	839	◪		⦚	360	beige brown
U	840				379	lt beige brown
☆	931	◪			1034	dk grey blue
$	932	◪			1033	grey blue
◇	962	◪		⦚	75	pink
◼	3021	◪		⦚	905	dk grey brown
♥	3023					grey brown
4	3024	◪			397	lt grey brown
●	3064	⦚			883	flesh
	3350			⦚	59	dk pink
◼	3371	◪			382	vy dk brown
✳	3687	◪	▨		68	dk mauve
★	3688	◪			66	mauve
+	3689	◪			49	lt mauve
▨	Grey area indicates first row of right section of design.					

The design was stitched over 2 fabric threads on a 19" x 16" piece of Delicate Teal Jobelan (28 ct). Two strands of floss were used for Cross Stitch and 1 strand for Half Cross Stitch and Backstitch. It was custom framed.

Design by Betty Morris Hamilton.

149w x 112h

STAR-SPANGLED BEARS

Nothing brings Americans together like the love we have for our country. Adapted for cross stitch from a watercolor print, this all-American portrait was inspired by the show of patriotism during the Persian Gulf crisis. The flag-waving bears pay tribute to all the men and women who have served our great nation.

For Sentimental Reasons

We cherish our favorite teddies for sentimental reasons — usually each one reminds us of someone we hold dear or of a day that's linked to loving memories. This collection honors those emotions and experiences that make our lives more fulfilling. In this sweet design, a wagonload of cubs portrays a timeless message about a mother's love.

love will pull us through...

94w x 75h

a mother's love will pull us through...

The design was stitched on a 14" x 13" piece of Ivory Aida (14 ct). Three strands of floss were used for Cross Stitch and 1 strand for Backstitch and French Knots. If desired, sew a 1⅛" dia. black button on top of wheel. It was made into a pillow.

For pillow, trim stitched piece 1¼" larger on all sides than design. Cut one piece of fabric same size as stitched piece for backing.

For ruffle, press short ends of a 5" x 56" strip of fabric ½" to wrong side. Matching wrong sides and long edges, fold strip in half; press. Gather fabric strip to fit pillow. Matching raw edges and beginning at bottom edge, pin ruffle to right side of stitched piece, overlapping short ends ¼"; use a ½" seam allowance to baste ruffle to stitched piece. Matching right sides and leaving an opening for turning, use a ½" seam allowance and sew stitched piece and backing fabric together. Trim corners diagonally. Turn pillow right side out, carefully pushing corners outward. Stuff pillow with polyester fiberfill and sew final closure by hand.

Design by Kathie Rueger.

X	DMC	¼X	B'ST	ANC.	COLOR
•	blanc			2	white
O	ecru			387	ecru
•	310		/	403	black
X	347			1025	red
+	434			310	dk brown
•	435			1046	brown
*	436			1045	lt brown
S	561			212	green
C	738			361	vy lt brown
☆	760			1022	dk pink
V	761			1021	pink
■	816			1005	dk red
–	898		/	360	vy dk brown
★	931			1034	dk blue
2	932			1033	blue
✿	3328			1024	lt red
⊙	310	black French Knot			

36

It's often said that a true friend is one who knows everything about you — and likes you anyway! This insightful design will make a sweet token of affection for someone who's been a blessing to you.

The design was stitched on an 11" x 9" piece of Ivory Aida (14 ct). Two strands of floss were used for Cross Stitch and 1 strand for Backstitch and French Knots. It was inserted in a mini towel rack frame (6¾" x 4½" opening).

Design by Debra Jordan Meyer for Fraser & Co.

58w x 50h

a true friend
is a
rare
blessing

X	DMC	¼X	B'ST	ANC.	COLOR
•	ecru	·		387	ecru
U	415			398	grey
●	434			310	dk tan
X	435			1046	tan
C	436			1045	lt tan
5	502			877	green
•	503		·	876	lt green
V	504			1042	vy lt green
–	738			361	vy lt tan
4	754			1012	peach
•	758		·	882	dk peach
●	760			1022	rose
△	761			1021	lt rose
P	842			388	beige
H	931			1034	blue
O	932			1033	lt blue
2	976			1001	copper
●	977			1002	lt copper
+	3024			397	taupe
▲	3328			1024	dk rose
◆	3371		∕	382	brown
●	503				lt green French Knot
•	3371				brown French Knot

Share a little sunshine with someone who's touched your life by presenting them with this heartwarming design. The sincere message is sure to brighten their day!

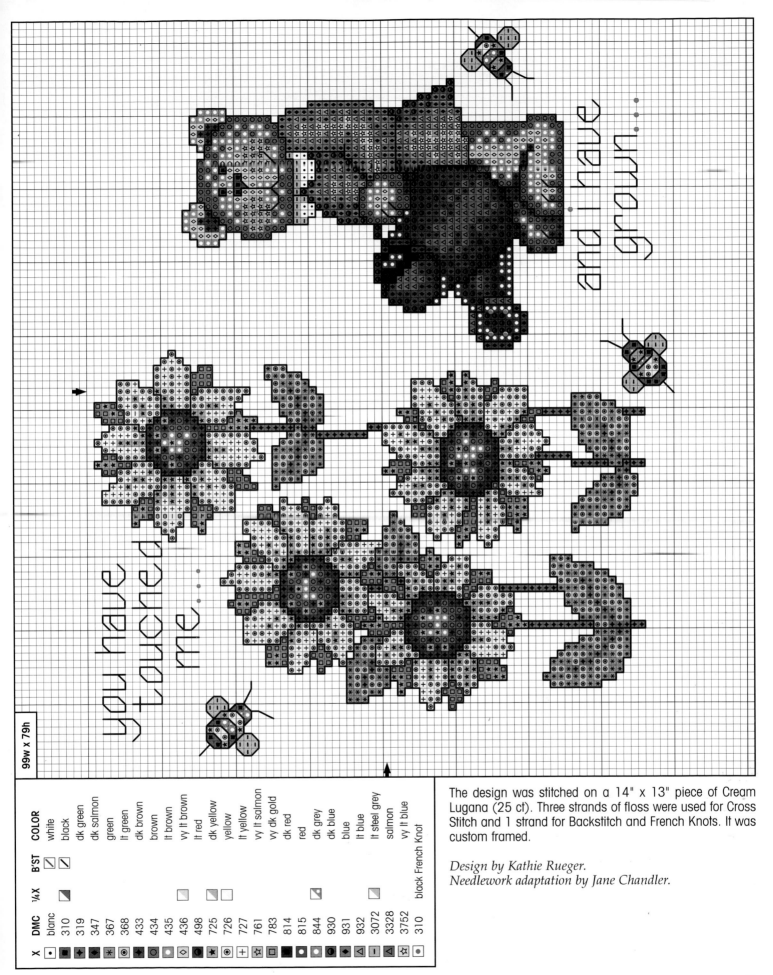

The design was stitched on a 14" x 13" piece of Cream Lugana (25 ct). Three strands of floss were used for Cross Stitch and 1 strand for Backstitch and French Knots. It was custom framed.

Design by Kathie Rueger.
Needlework adaptation by Jane Chandler.

X	DMC	¼X	B'ST	COLOR
·	blanc			white
■	310		◪ ◪	black
★	319			dk green
◆	347			dk salmon
✳	367			green
◉	368			lt green
◐	433			dk brown
○	434		◪	brown
◇	435		◪	lt brown
◓	436		◪	vy lt brown
★	498			lt red
◉	725			dk yellow
+	726			yellow
☆	727			lt yellow
□	761			vy lt salmon
■	783			vy dk gold
◐	814			dk red
●	815		◪	red
◑	844			dk grey
◆	930			dk blue
◁	931			blue
	932			lt blue
◁	3072		◪	lt steel grey
☆	3328			salmon
◉	3752			vy lt blue
	310			black French Knot

39

Touching moments like a big bear hug from Mom and a game of "ride the horsey" with Dad are what make parents dear to us. These unforgettable scenes are captured on mugs that let parents know they're the best!

54w x 44h

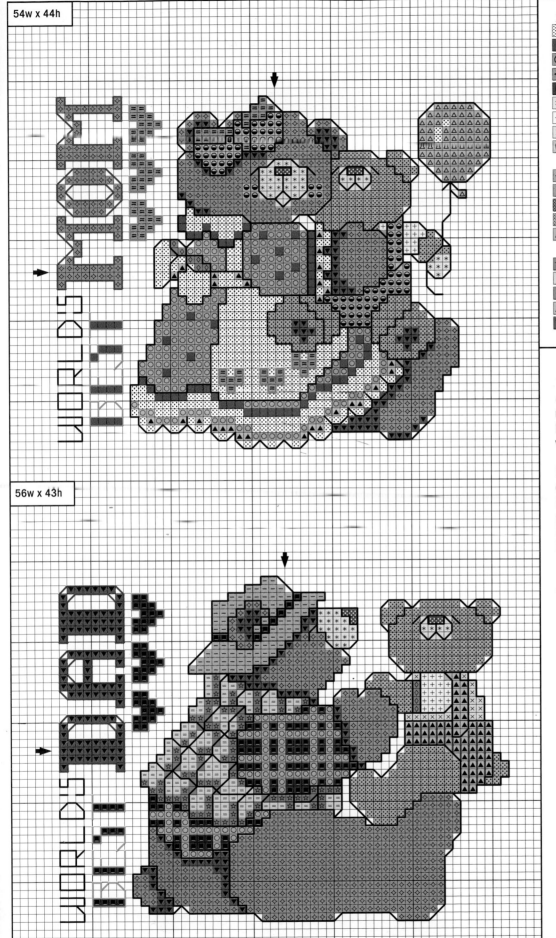

56w x 43h

X	DMC	B'ST	ANC.	COLOR
▨	blanc		2	white
■	309	╱	42	dk pink
○	310	╱	403	black
◇	402		1047	rust
■	666	╱	46	red
✳	739		387	tan
+	743		302	yellow
✕	745		300	lt yellow
◒	770		24	lt pink
	798	╱	131	dk blue
⊟	841		378	beige
=	899		52	pink
▨	938		381	dk brown
▨	945		881	lt rust
△	955		206	yellow green
	975	╱	355	brown
★	3012		844	green
=	3013		842	lt green
◇	3325		129	blue
▲	3753		1031	lt blue
▼	3776		1048	dk rust

Each design was stitched on a 10¼" x 3½" piece of Vinyl-Weave™ (14 ct). Three strands of floss were used for Cross Stitch and 1 strand for Backstitch. They were inserted in white mugs.

For design placement, fold vinyl in half, matching short edges. Center design on right half of vinyl if mug is to be used by a right-handed person or on the left half if mug is to be used by a left-handed person. Hand wash mug to protect stitchery.

Design by Linda Gillum.

41

AFTERNOON TEA

This timeless scene brings to mind the childhood tea parties we shared with teddy bears and dolls.

Like a cherished teddy bear, the lessons we learn in Sunday school stick with us for a lifetime. We share two of our favorite scriptures — and some lovable bears — in this inspirational pair of designs.

...he which soweth bounti- fully shall reap also bountifully. II Corinthians 9:6

Let your light so shine before men, that they may see your good works, and glorify your Father in heaven. Matthew 5:16

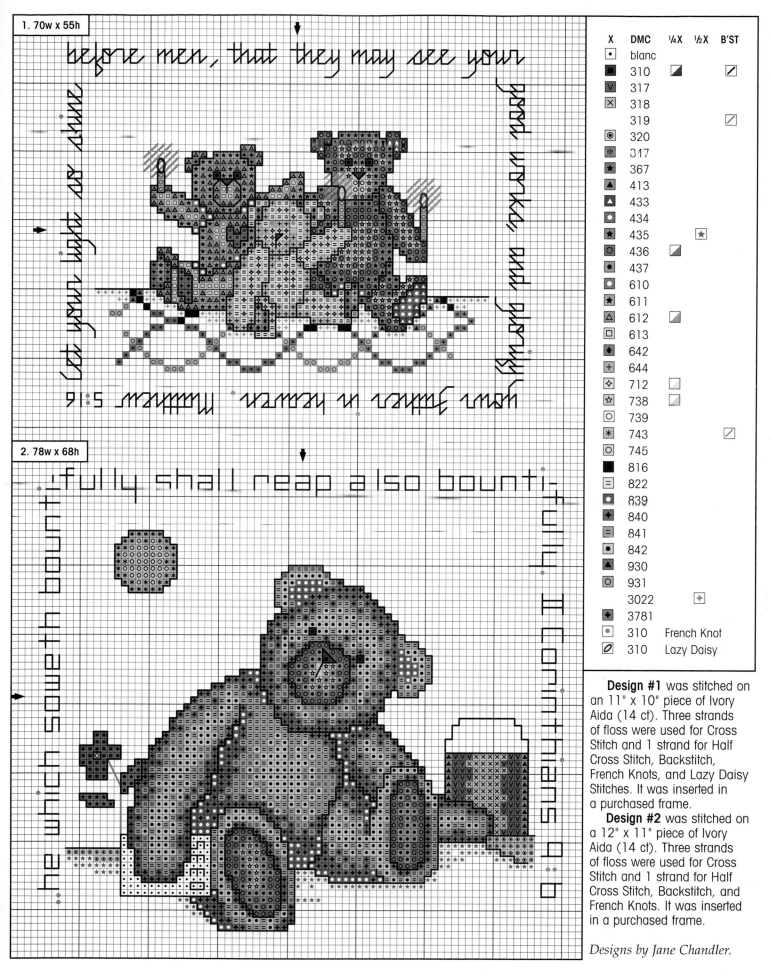

1. 70w x 55h

before men, that they may see your

good works, and glorify

Let your light so shine

your Father in heaven. Matthew 5:16

2. 78w x 68h

...fully shall reap also bounti-

-fully. II Corinthians 9:6

he which soweth bounti-

X	DMC	¼X	½X	B'ST
⊡	blanc			
■	310	◪		◪
V	317			
⊠	318			
	319			◪
◉	320			
⊞	317			
★	367			
▲	413			
▲	433			
◧	434			
★	435		★	
◎	436	◪		
●	437			
⊡	610			
★	611			
△	612	◪		
⊡	613			
◆	642			
+	644			
⬖	712	◪		
☆	738	◪		
◯	739			
✳	743			◪
◯	745			
◉	822			
◘	839			
◆	840			
=	841			
●	842			
▲	930			
◎	931			
	3022		◆	
◆	3781			
⊙	310	French Knot		
⊘	310	Lazy Daisy		

Design #1 was stitched on an 11" x 10" piece of Ivory Aida (14 ct). Three strands of floss were used for Cross Stitch and 1 strand for Half Cross Stitch, Backstitch, French Knots, and Lazy Daisy Stitches. It was inserted in a purchased frame.

Design #2 was stitched on a 12" x 11" piece of Ivory Aida (14 ct). Three strands of floss were used for Cross Stitch and 1 strand for Half Cross Stitch, Backstitch, and French Knots. It was inserted in a purchased frame.

Designs by Jane Chandler.

The times we spend with friends and family in our homes are often some of the happiest moments in our lives. Displayed in your entryway, this cheery design will let special people know they're always welcome.

48

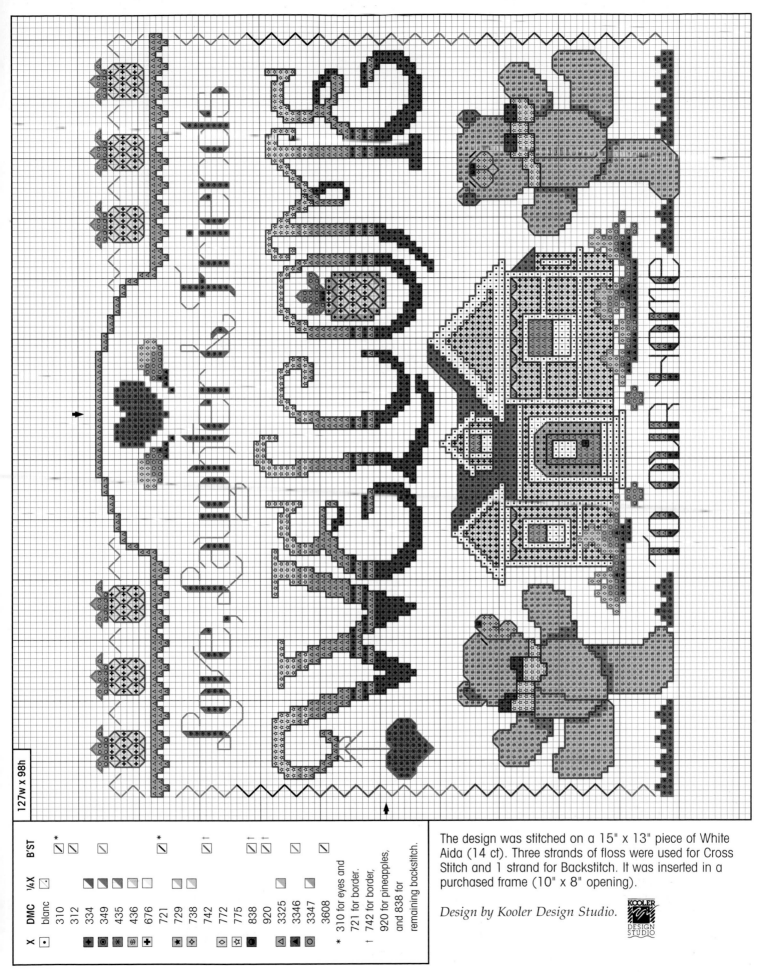

127w x 98h

The design was stitched on a 15" x 13" piece of White Aida (14 ct). Three strands of floss were used for Cross Stitch and 1 strand for Backstitch. It was inserted in a purchased frame (10" x 8" opening).

Design by Kooler Design Studio.

KOOLER
DESIGN
STUDIO

X	1/4X	B'ST	DMC	
·	·	*	blanc	
		☑ ☑	310	
		☑	312	
★	◪		334	
⊙	◪	* ☑	349	
✳	◪		435	
⊞	◪		436	
✚	◻	† ☑	676	
		†	721	
★		† ☑	729	
✧	◪	† ☑	738	
	◪	☑	742	
◇			772	
⊙			775	
◉		☑	838	
◨	◻		920	
◨	◻		3325	
◀			3346	
◧	◻		3347	
			3608	

* 310 for eyes and 721 for border.
† 742 for border, 920 for pineapples, and 838 for remaining backstitch.

Priscilla and her little friend Ben are all dressed up and ready for a day filled with adventure! The fun-loving twosome will look especially charming when paired with Kindred Spirits on page 52.

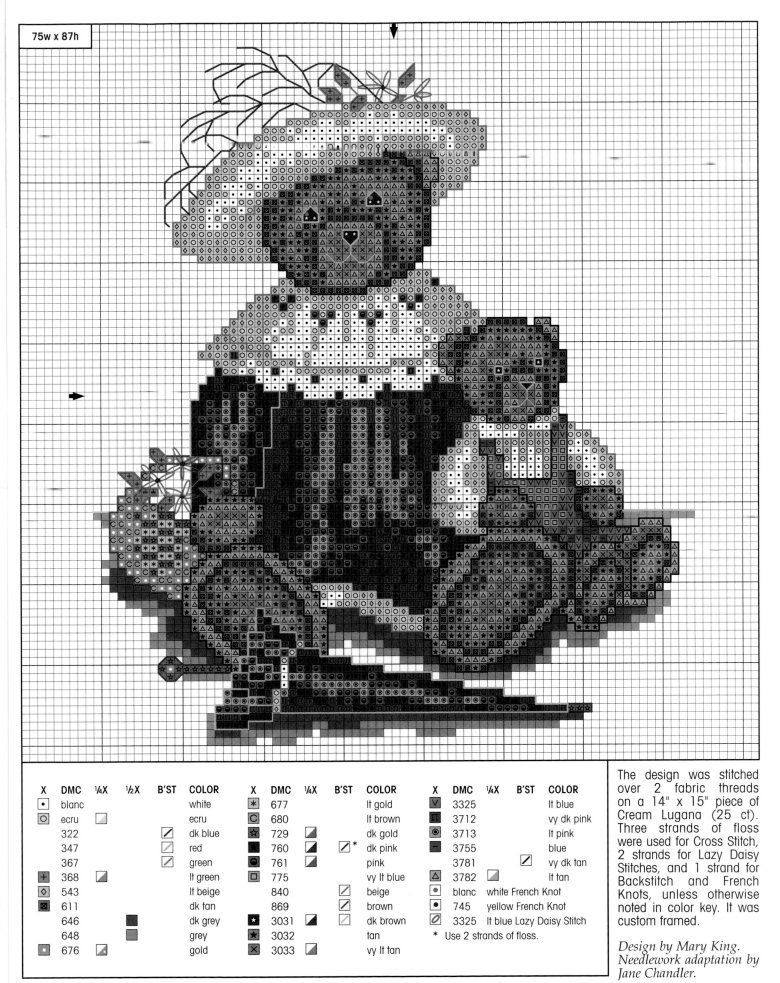

75w x 87h

X	DMC	¼X	½X	B'ST	COLOR	X	DMC	¼X	B'ST	COLOR	X	DMC	¼X	B'ST	COLOR
•	blanc				white	*	677			lt gold	V	3325			lt blue
⊙	ecru	◹			ecru	C	680			lt brown	⊞	3712			vy dk pink
	322			◿	dk blue	☆	729	◹		dk gold	⊙	3713			lt pink
	347			◿	red	●	760	◹	◿ *	dk pink	–	3755			blue
	367			◿	green	◖	761	◹		pink		3781		◿	vy dk tan
+	368	◹			lt green	⬚	775			vy lt blue	△	3782	◹		lt tan
◇	543				lt beige		840		◿	beige	•	blanc			white French Knot
⊠	611				dk tan		869		◿	brown	•	745			yellow French Knot
	646		■		dk grey	★	3031		◿	dk brown	⊘	3325			lt blue Lazy Daisy Stitch
	648		▣		grey	★	3032			tan					
⊡	676	◹			gold	X	3033	◹		vy lt tan		* Use 2 strands of floss.			

The design was stitched over 2 fabric threads on a 14" x 15" piece of Cream Lugana (25 ct). Three strands of floss were used for Cross Stitch, 2 strands for Lazy Daisy Stitches, and 1 strand for Backstitch and French Knots, unless otherwise noted in color key. It was custom framed.

Design by Mary King. Needlework adaptation by Jane Chandler.

51

> *Love-worn teddy bears, quilts, and little red wagons are always in the picture when we make a list of our favorite things.*

X	DMC	1/4X	1/2X	B'ST	COLOR	X	DMC	1/4X	COLOR	X	DMC	1/4X	COLOR
●	310	◪		◪	black	–	500		green	+	841	◪	beige
■	321				red	★	642		tan	●	842		lt beige
■	336				blue	●	644	◪	lt tan	2	902		dk maroon
★	414				dk grey brown	○	739		vy lt beige	S	3022		grey brown
◉	434			◪	dk gold	+	814		maroon	Σ	3023		lt grey brown
✦	435		▢		gold	◉	816		lt maroon	☆	3024	◪	vy lt grey brown
◆	436		▢		lt gold	▲	839		vy dk beige	C	3790		dk tan
✕	437	▢	▢		vy lt gold	●	840		dk beige	●	310		black French Knot

The design was stitched on a 16" square of Ivory Aida (14 ct). Three strands of floss were used for Cross Stitch and 1 strand for Half Cross Stitch, Backstitch, and French Knots. It was custom framed.

Design by Jane Chandler.

Little Teddy Bears

Children are "beary" special people — they fill our hearts with love and give our lives a sense of continued joy. These precious gifts from God are sweetly remembered in this touching collection. You'll find lots of treasures for baby, from afghans and bibs to a birth sampler and sipper cups. As your little ones grow, our Look What I Did! *design will let you proudly display their artwork or school papers. What a great way to nurture self-esteem!*

57

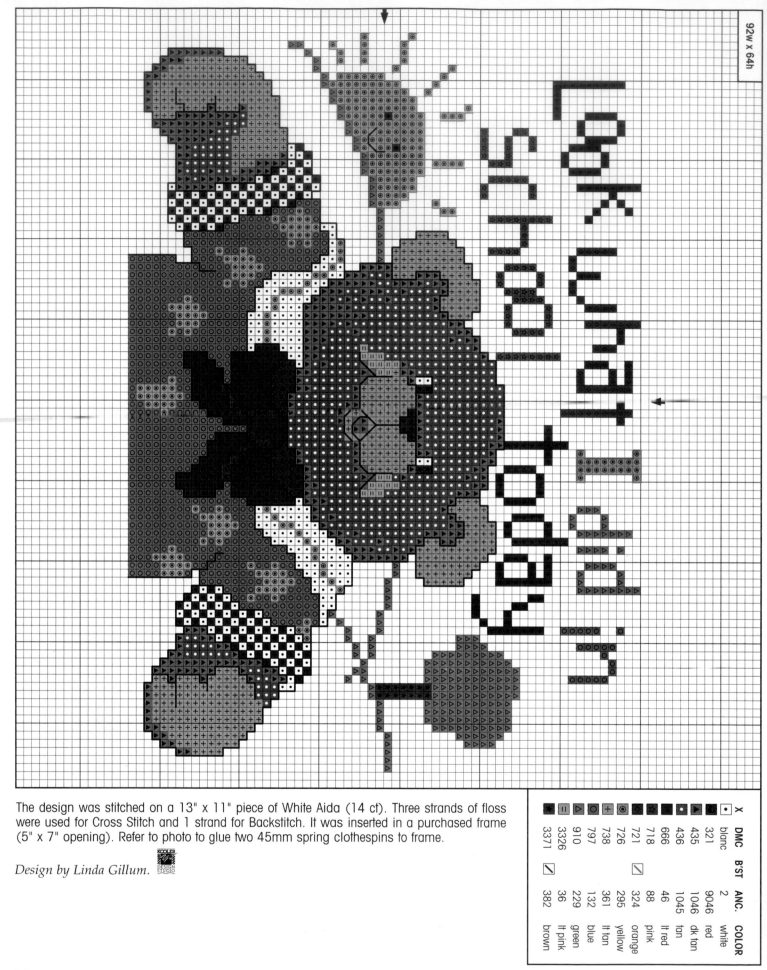

92w x 64h

The design was stitched on a 13" x 11" piece of White Aida (14 ct). Three strands of floss were used for Cross Stitch and 1 strand for Backstitch. It was inserted in a purchased frame (5" x 7" opening). Refer to photo to glue two 45mm spring clothespins to frame.

Design by Linda Gillum.

X	DMC	B'ST	ANC.	COLOR
●	blanc		2	white
‖	321		9046	red
▷	435		1046	dk tan
○	436		1045	tan
+	666		46	lt red
⊙	718		88	pink
❋	721		324	orange
✦	726		295	yellow
■	738		361	lt tan
◆	797		132	blue
▶	910	◢	229	green
■	3326		36	lt pink
□	3371	◢	382	brown

58

Embellishing a bib and sipper cup, this adorable teddy bear is almost as precious as your own little angel. The heavenly set will also make an ideal gift for a baby shower.

X	DMC	1/4X	B'ST	ANC.	COLOR
•	blanc	⧅		2	white
	349		⧄	13	red
◆	352			9	dk peach
=	353			6	peach
✳	435			1046	dk tan
◇	437			362	tan
✕	554			96	purple
☆	563			208	green
○	564			206	lt green
•	739			387	lt tan
+	754			1012	lt peach
△	760			1022	pink
V	775	⧄		128	lt blue
	898		⧄	360	brown
	3755		⧄	140	blue
⊙	898		brown French Knot		

Design by Lorri Birmingham.

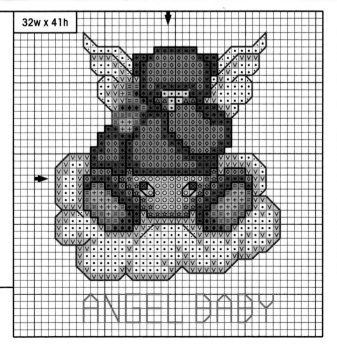

32w x 41h

The entire design was centered and stitched on a white Aida (14 ct) baby bib. Three strands of floss were used for Cross Stitch and 1 strand for Backstitch and French Knots.

Baby and Cloud only were stitched (omitting Quarter Stitches) on a 7½" x 3" piece of Vinyl-Weave™ (14 ct). Three strands of floss were used for Cross Stitch and 1 strand for Backstitch and French Knots. It was inserted in a Stitch-A-Sipper™. Hand wash to protect stitchery.

LOVING LESSONS

Anyone who loves children will be inspired by these "beary" gentle proverbs. Displayed in a frame, the lessons of love will provide a daily reminder of how important it is to guide and cherish our children.

The best thing to spend on a child is TIME

CHILDREN LEARN TO LOVE BY BEING LOVED

Children need love when they least deserve it.

a child is Gods most precious gift.

Two gifts we can give our children: roots and wings

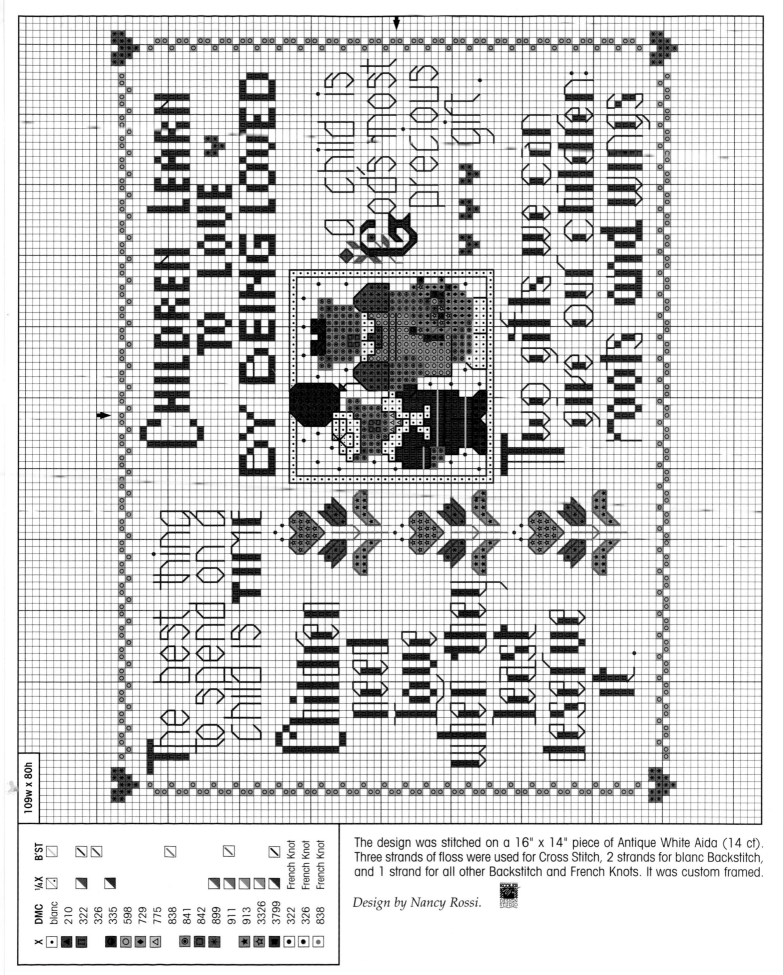

The design was stitched on a 16" x 14" piece of Antique White Aida (14 ct). Three strands of floss were used for Cross Stitch, 2 strands for blanc Backstitch, and 1 strand for all other Backstitch and French Knots. It was custom framed.

Design by Nancy Rossi.

61

Score a touchdown with your little football fan when you present him with this terrific tee! Wearing our geared-up bear, he'll be ready to tackle the world.

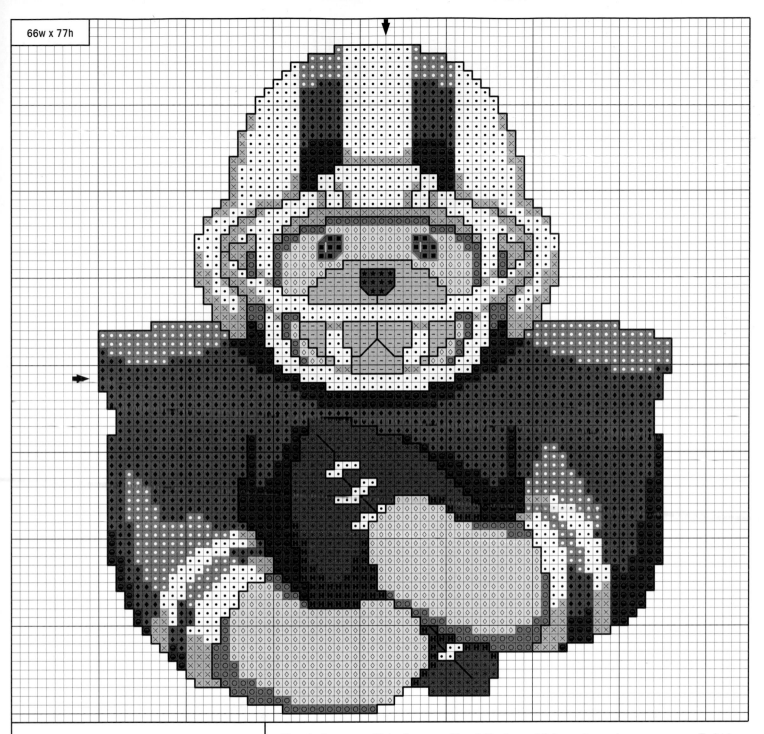

66w x 77h

X	DMC	¼X	B'ST	ANC.	COLOR
•	blanc		⟋ *	2	white
▉	300			352	dk rust
✳	301			1049	rust
▩	310	◢	⟋	403	black
◆	321			9046	red
✕	415			398	grey
★	433	◢		358	brown
◎	435			1046	lt brown
◇	437		◱	362	tan
⬤	498			1005	dk red
⦿	666			46	lt red
⁃	739		◲	387	lt tan
	938		⟋	381	dk brown

* Use 2 strands of floss.

The design was stitched over a 9" x 10" piece of 14 mesh waste canvas on a T-shirt. Three strands of floss were used for Cross Stitch and 1 strand for Backstitch unless otherwise noted in color key. See Working on Waste Canvas, page 143.

Design by Holly DeFount.

With their high energy and enthusiasm, children make natural cheerleaders. A purchased dress stitched with our exuberant bear will encourage your little miss to excel at any activity.

90w x 85h

X	DMC	¼X	B'ST	ANC.	COLOR
•	blanc			2	white
◢	208			110	dk lavender
2	210			108	lavender
✕	415			398	lt grey
★	433	◢		358	dk brown
◎	435	◢		1046	brown
◇	437			362	tan
=	739	◢		387	lt tan
	938		◢	381	vy dk brown
✳	957	◢		50	rose
◉	963	◢		73	lt rose

The design was stitched over an 11" x 10" piece of 14 mesh waste canvas on a dress. Three strands of floss were used for Cross Stitch and 1 strand for Backstitch. See Working on Waste Canvas, page 143.

Design by Holly DeFount.

This whimsical birth sampler is as simple to make as A-B-C. And who better than a lovable, huggable teddy to announce baby's arrival!

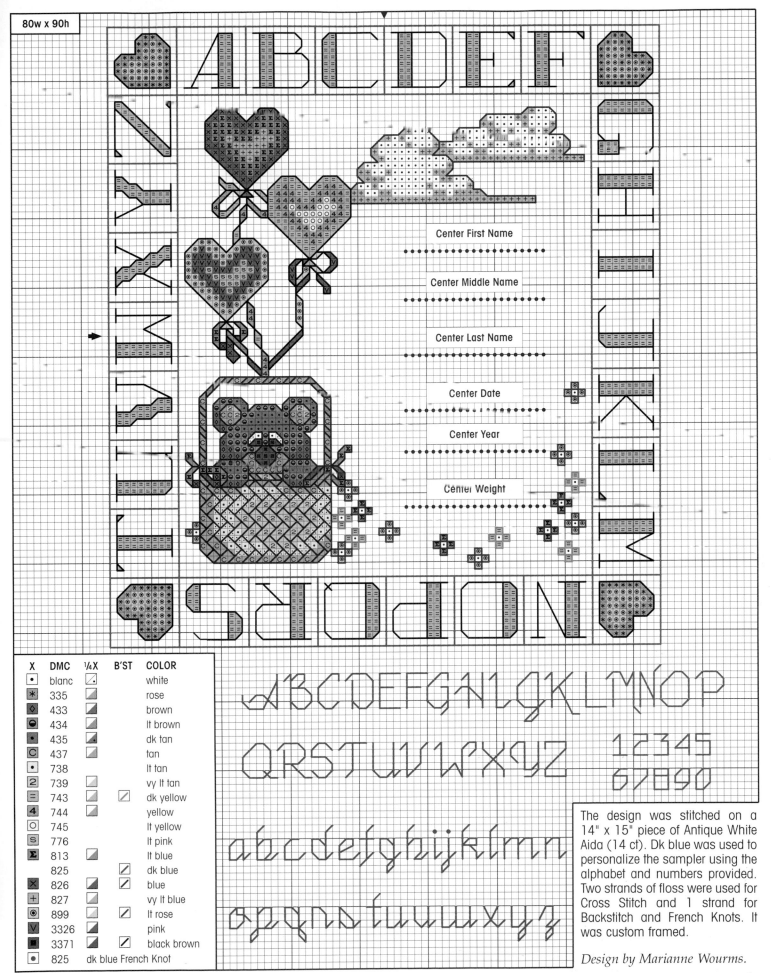

80w x 90h

X	DMC	¼X	B'ST	COLOR
•	blanc			white
*	335			rose
◇	433			brown
⊖	434			lt brown
•	435			dk tan
C	437			tan
•	738			lt tan
2	739			vy lt tan
=	743		✓	dk yellow
4	744			yellow
O	745			lt yellow
S	776			lt pink
Σ	813			lt blue
	825		✓	dk blue
✕	826		✓	blue
+	827			vy lt blue
⊙	899		✓	lt rose
V	3326			pink
■	3371		✓	black brown
•	825			dk blue French Knot

Center First Name

Center Middle Name

Center Last Name

Center Date

Center Year

Center Weight

The design was stitched on a 14" x 15" piece of Antique White Aida (14 ct). Dk blue was used to personalize the sampler using the alphabet and numbers provided. Two strands of floss were used for Cross Stitch and 1 strand for Backstitch and French Knots. It was custom framed.

Design by Marianne Wourms.

Reminiscent of a fairy tale, this exquisite illustration showcases a baby teddy bear sailing through a sea of clouds. The enchanting afghan and framed piece will bring the magic of make-believe to life for you and a little one.

91w x 135h

The entire design was stitched over 2 fabric threads on a 17" x 20" piece of Antique White Lugana (25 ct). Three strands of floss were used for Cross Stitch and 1 strand for Half Cross Stitch, Backstitch, French Knots, and Lazy Daisy Stitches. It was custom framed.

A portion of the design (refer to photo) was stitched over 2 fabric threads on a 29" x 45" piece (baby afghan size) of White All-Cotton Anne Cloth (18 ct). Six strands of floss were used for Cross Stitch and 2 strands for Backstitch, French Knots, and Lazy Daisy Stitches. It was made into an afghan. Refer to Diagram for placement of design on fabric.

X	B'ST	1/4X	DMC	ANC.	COLOR
			913	204	green
			958	187	dk aqua
			959	186	aqua
			964	185	lt aqua
			3024	397	lt beige grey
			3755	140	blue
			3821		gold
			3822		lt gold
			3823		lt yellow
			blanc		white French Knot
			910		dk green Lazy Daisy Stitch

Grey area indicates last row of top section of design.

X	B'ST	1/4X	DMC	ANC.	COLOR
			543	933	cream
			645	273	beige grey
			738	361	tan
			739	387	lt tan
			742	303	lt orange
			743	302	dk yellow
			744	301	yellow
			762	234	lt grey
			775	128	lt blue
			776	24	lt pink
			818	23	vy lt pink
			844	1041	dk beige grey
			899	52	pink
			910	229	dk green

X	1/4X	1/2X	DMC	B'ST	ANC.	COLOR
			blanc		2	white
			ecru		387	ecru
			208		110	dk purple
			209		109	purple
			210		108	lt purple
			211		342	vy lt purple
			310		403	black
			335		38	dk pink
			415		398	grey
			433		358	dk brown
			434		310	brown
			435		1046	lt brown
			437		362	dk tan
			519		1038	blue green

For afghan, cut selvages from fabric. Machine stitch along raised threads around outside edge of afghan. Fringe fabric to machine-stitched lines.

Design by Carol Bryan. the fraser collection
Needlework adaptation by Jane Chandler.

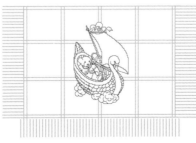

Tenderhearted teddy bears make wonderful companions for even the smallest of children. These designs add playful touches to accessories for baby, including an afghan, a bib, a mug, and a sweatshirt.

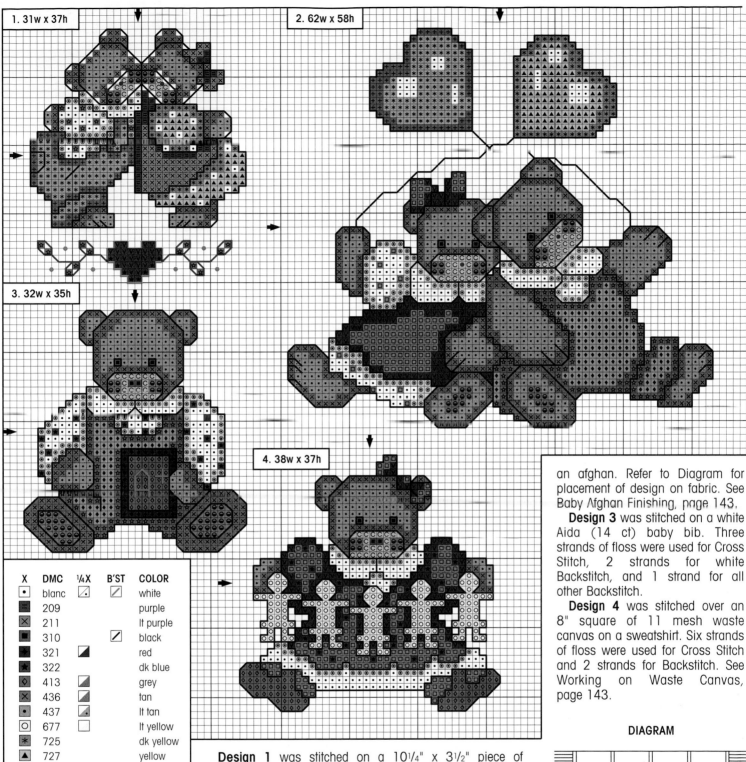

1. 31w x 37h

2. 62w x 58h

3. 32w x 35h

4. 38w x 37h

X	DMC	¼X	B'ST	COLOR
•	blanc	◢	◢	white
▤	209			purple
✕	211			lt purple
■	310		◢	black
★	321	◢		red
★	322			dk blue
◆	413	◢		grey
✕	436	◢		tan
•	437	◢		lt tan
○	677	◻		lt yellow
✳	725			dk yellow
▲	727			yellow
C	739	◢		vy lt tan
●	760	◢		salmon
✳	800			lt blue
+	809			blue
★	899		◢	dk rose
☆	954	◢	◢	green
◆	955			lt green
▢	963			lt rose
◩	3326	◢		rose
◉	3753	◻		vy lt blue
◉	310			black French Knot
◉	899			dk rose French Knot

Design 1 was stitched on a 10¼" x 3½" piece of Vinyl-Weave™ (14 ct). Three strands of floss were used for Cross Stitch and 1 strand for Backstitch and French Knots. It was inserted in a white mug.

For design placement, fold vinyl in half, matching short edges. Center design on right half of vinyl if mug is to be used by a right-handed person or on the left half if mug is to be used by a left-handed person. Hand wash mug to protect stitchery.

Design 2 was stitched over 2 fabric threads on a 29" x 45" piece (baby afghan size) of Soft White Anne Cloth (18 ct). Six strands of floss were used for Cross Stitch and 2 strands for Backstitch and French Knots. It was made into

an afghan. Refer to Diagram for placement of design on fabric. See Baby Afghan Finishing, page 143.

Design 3 was stitched on a white Aida (14 ct) baby bib. Three strands of floss were used for Cross Stitch, 2 strands for white Backstitch, and 1 strand for all other Backstitch.

Design 4 was stitched over an 8" square of 11 mesh waste canvas on a sweatshirt. Six strands of floss were used for Cross Stitch and 2 strands for Backstitch. See Working on Waste Canvas, page 143.

DIAGRAM

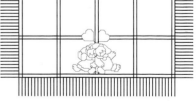

Designs by Lorraine Birmingham.

Handy for back-to-school, these nifty tote bags are just right for carrying a child's favorite things. The sturdy carryalls are sure to get high marks from your little student — especially when they're accented with one of our delightful designs for boys or girls.

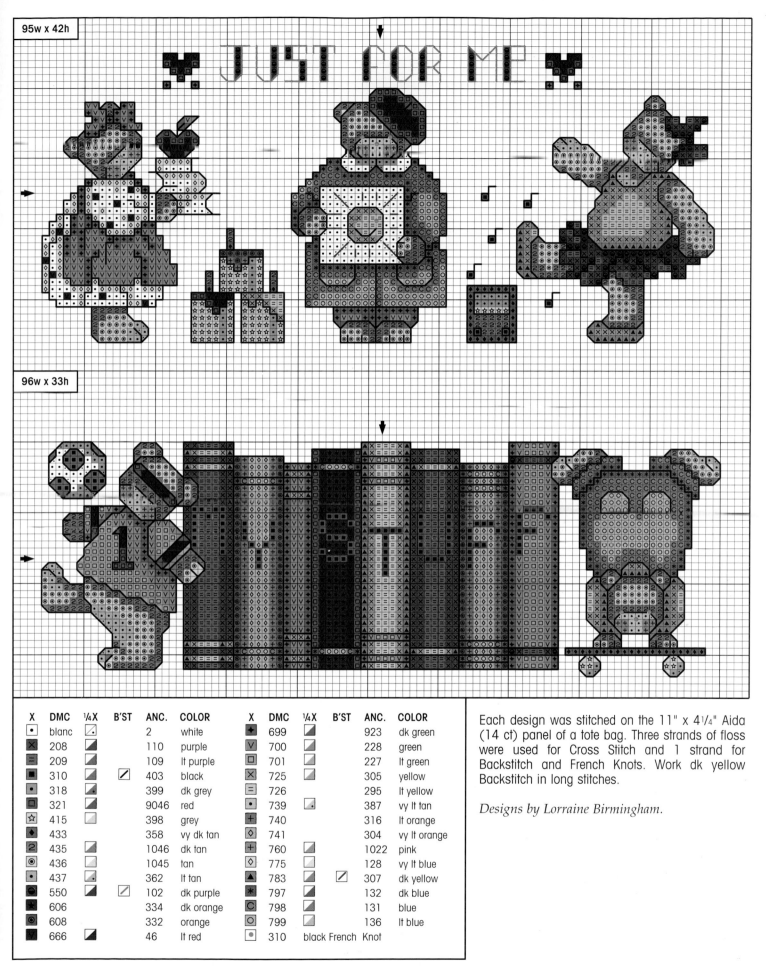

X	DMC	¼X	B'ST	ANC.	COLOR	X	DMC	¼X	B'ST	ANC.	COLOR
•	blanc			2	white		699			923	dk green
✕	208			110	purple	V	700			228	green
=	209			109	lt purple	□	701			227	lt green
■	310		✓	403	black	✕	725			305	yellow
•	318			399	dk grey	=	726			295	lt yellow
□	321			9046	red	•	739			387	vy lt tan
☆	415			398	grey	+	740			316	lt orange
◆	433			358	vy dk tan	◇	741			304	vy lt orange
2	435			1046	dk tan	+	760			1022	pink
⊙	436			1045	tan	◇	775			128	vy lt blue
•	437			362	lt tan	▲	783		✓	307	dk yellow
●	550		✓	102	dk purple	✳	797			132	dk blue
★	606			334	dk orange	C	798			131	blue
⊙	608			332	orange	O	799			136	lt blue
■	666			46	lt red	⊙	310				black French Knot

Each design was stitched on the 11" x 4¼" Aida (14 ct) panel of a tote bag. Three strands of floss were used for Cross Stitch and 1 strand for Backstitch and French Knots. Work dk yellow Backstitch in long stitches.

Designs by Lorraine Birmingham.

Want to add a bit of fun to baby's mealtime? This bib and towel set features a friendly panda before and after he's enjoyed his wagonload of fruits and vegetables.

X	DMC	¼X	B'ST	ANC.	COLOR
•	blanc			2	white
S	209			109	purple
✕	309			42	dk pink
◖	310		✓	403	black
△	437			362	tan
+	744			301	dk yellow
○	745			300	yellow
◉	776			24	pink
◆	913			204	dk green
☆	955			206	green
✳	3325			129	blue
★	3340			329	dk peach
–	3341			328	peach

1. 64w x 27h

2. 68w x 27h

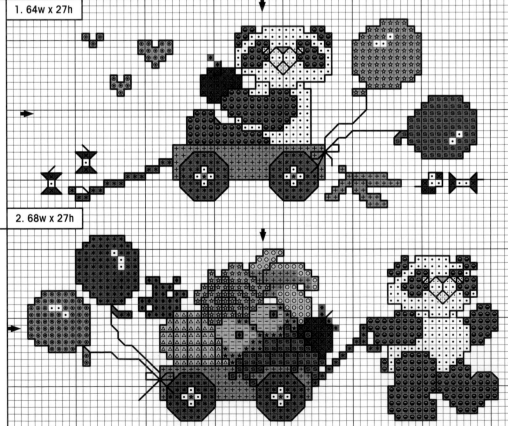

Design 1 was stitched on the 14 ct insert of a white fingertip towel. Three strands of floss were used for Cross Stitch and 1 strand for Backstitch.

Design 2 was stitched on the 14 ct insert of a white baby bib. Three strands of floss were used for Cross Stitch and 1 strand for Backstitch.

Designs by Linda Gillum.

78

Playfully posed on blocks that spell out the word "Baby," these frolicking cubs make a sweet design for the nursery.

Beary Happy Holidays

Celebrating the holidays is more fun when you share the time with friends. And who better than an old chum like Teddy to make special occasions merrier! This fun assortment of designs celebrates all our favorite holidays from Valentine's Day to Christmas. You'll find a variety of projects, too, such as ornaments, a sweater, a wall hanging, and more. An artistic bear dazzles us with his "sweet" designs on an afghan in Candy Cane Red.

Very Vogue Teddies

Teddy bears have been in vogue since they were first introduced in the early 1900's. To celebrate the enduring popularity of the cuddly toy, we've created a whole collection of wonderful wearables. You'll find adorable items for grownups as well as youngsters and babies. The humorous sentiment on this "Beary" Cute Shirt makes it a great choice for wearing on your birthday. These embellished fashions will capture your heart!

i wish i
were a
teddy
BEAR
the older
they get,
the more
they're
worth...

X	DMC	¼X	B'ST	ANC.	COLOR	X	DMC	¼X	B'ST	ANC.	COLOR
▲	310	◪	◪	403	black	☆	739	◪		387	lt tan
★	433			358	dk brown	◐	761			1021	pink
●	434			310	brown	◉	844			1041	grey
✳	435			1046	lt brown	◗	930		◪	1035	blue
△	436	◪		1045	dk tan	•	310				black French Knot
=	712	◪		926	vy lt tan	●	930				blue French Knot
•	738	◪		361	tan						

The design was stitched over an 11" x 13" piece of 10 mesh waste canvas on a sweatshirt. Six strands of floss were used for Cross Stitch, 3 strands for 930 Backstitch and French Knots, and 2 strands for 310 Backstitch and French Knots. See Working on Waste Canvas, page 143.

Design by Kathie Rueger.
Needlework adaptation by Jane Chandler.

72w x 86h

A BEARABLE RESOLUTION

To inspire you to make and keep a New Year's resolution to exercise, why not stitch this playful sweatshirt. It'll make working out a little more bearable!

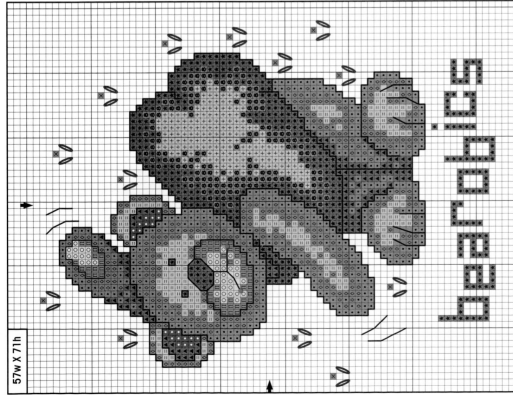

X	DMC	ANC.	COLOR
★	310	403	black
✕	335	38	pink
╈	413	401	grey
◢	433	358	vy dk brown
◀	434	310	dk brown
◆	435	1046	brown
‖	436	1045	lt brown
⊓	437	362	vy lt brown
○	738	361	tan
◉	739	387	lt tan
●	3799	236	dk grey
◢	310		black French Knot
⌀	561		green Lazy Daisy Stitch

B'ST: ◹ 310 403 black

¼X: ◹ 433 358, ◹ 434 310, ◹ 739 387

57w X 71h

The design was stitched over an 11" x 13" piece of 8.5 mesh waste canvas on a sweatshirt. Six strands of floss were used for Cross Stitch and 2 strands for Backstitch, French Knots, and Lazy Daisy Stitches. See Working on Waste Canvas, page 143.

Design by Kathie Rueger.

This "bee-coming" shirt is something to buzz about! Clad in a clever disguise, our brave little bear carries a hive of delicious honey.

The design was stitched over a 12" x 14" piece of 8.5 mesh waste canvas on a T-shirt. Six strands of floss were used for Cross Stitch, 2 strands for Backstitch, and 3 strands for French Knots. See Working on Waste Canvas, page 143. Refer to photo to attach button to garment.

Design by Kathie Rueger. Needlework adaptation by Jane Chandler.

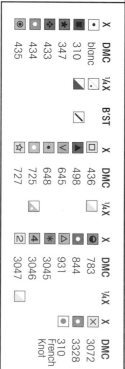

X	1/4X	B'ST		DMC		
◉	◐			310		
◻				blanc		
✦				347		
✦	◣			433		
◼				434		
•				435		

X	1/4X		DMC
☆	◢		436
◐	◢		498
•			645
◀			648
▶			725
◻			727

X	1/4X		DMC
2			783
4			844
✳			931
▷			3045
●			3046
◕			3047

X	DMC
●	3072
◻	3328
⊠	310 French Knot

66w x 87h

Dress baby in style with these adorable sweatshirts. The bubbly bears are perfect for playtime or mealtime!

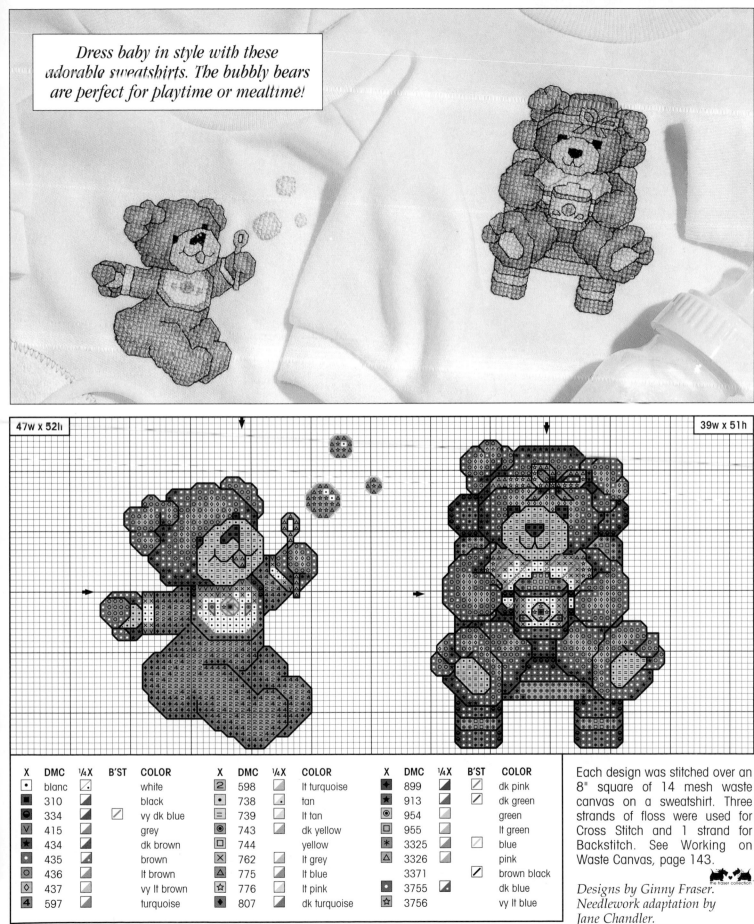

47w x 52h

39w x 51h

X	DMC	¼X	B'ST	COLOR	X	DMC	¼X	COLOR	X	DMC	¼X	B'ST	COLOR
•	blanc	◢		white	2	598	◢	lt turquoise	✦	899	◢	◢	dk pink
■	310	◢		black	•	738	◢	tan	★	913	◢	◢	dk green
◉	334	◢	◢	vy dk blue	=	739	◢	lt tan	◉	954	◢		green
V	415	◢		grey	◉	743	◢	dk yellow	□	955	◢		lt green
★	434	◢		dk brown	□	744	◢	yellow	✳	3325	◢	◢	blue
•	435	◢		brown	×	762	◢	lt grey	△	3326	◢		pink
◎	436	◢		lt brown	△	775	◢	lt blue		3371		◢	brown black
◇	437	◢		vy lt brown	☆	776	◢	lt pink	•	3755	◢		dk blue
4	597	◢		turquoise	◆	807	◢	dk turquoise	☆	3756	◢		vy lt blue

Each design was stitched over an 8" square of 14 mesh waste canvas on a sweatshirt. Three strands of floss were used for Cross Stitch and 1 strand for Backstitch. See Working on Waste Canvas, page 143.

Designs by Ginny Fraser. Needlework adaptation by Jane Chandler.

the fraser collection

The popularity of rummage sales inspired this whimsical sweatshirt design, which captures a trio of garage sale junkies toting their newfound treasures.

78w x 90h
GARAGE SALE
JUNKIE

X	DMC	¼X	B'ST	ANC.	COLOR	X	DMC	¼X	B'ST	ANC.	COLOR
•	blanc	◪		2	white	4	744	◪		301	yellow
■	310	◪	⁄	403	black	O	758	◪		882	peach
◉	318			399	dk grey	2	762			234	lt grey
+	351			10	pink	■	798			131	blue
=	415			398	grey		938		⁄	381	vy dk brown
✱	433			358	dk brown	+	964			185	aqua
◒	434	◪		310	brown	△	989			242	green
•	435	◪		1046	lt brown	■	3607			87	dk violet
+	437	◪		362	tan	V	3608			86	violet
★	470			267	dk yellow green	X	3609			85	lt violet
V	471			266	yellow green	▲	3778			1013	dk peach
2	472			253	lt yellow green	X	3779			868	lt peach
★*	553			98	purple	✪★	TH30002				
◒	554			96	lt purple	•	310				black French Knot
□	676			891	gold						
•†	676			891	gold						
✦	677			886	lt gold						
=	729	◪		890	dk gold						
•†	729			890	dk gold						
C	742			303	dk yellow						

* Use 6 strands of floss and 2 strands of Kreinik 012 purple Blending Filament.

† Use 6 strands of floss and 2 strands of Kreinik 002 gold Blending Filament.

★ Use 2 strands of True Colors International Silver Pre-Blended Thread, size 14.

The design was stitched over a 14" x 15" piece of 8.5 mesh waste canvas on a sweatshirt. Six strands of floss were used for Cross Stitch and 2 strands for Backstitch and French Knots, unless otherwise noted in color key. See Working on Waste Canvas, page 143.

Design by Karen Wood.

Cloaked in a kaleidoscope of brightly colored leaves, this free-spirited bear enjoys a playful autumn afternoon. To enhance the design, we stitched it on a forest green sweatshirt.

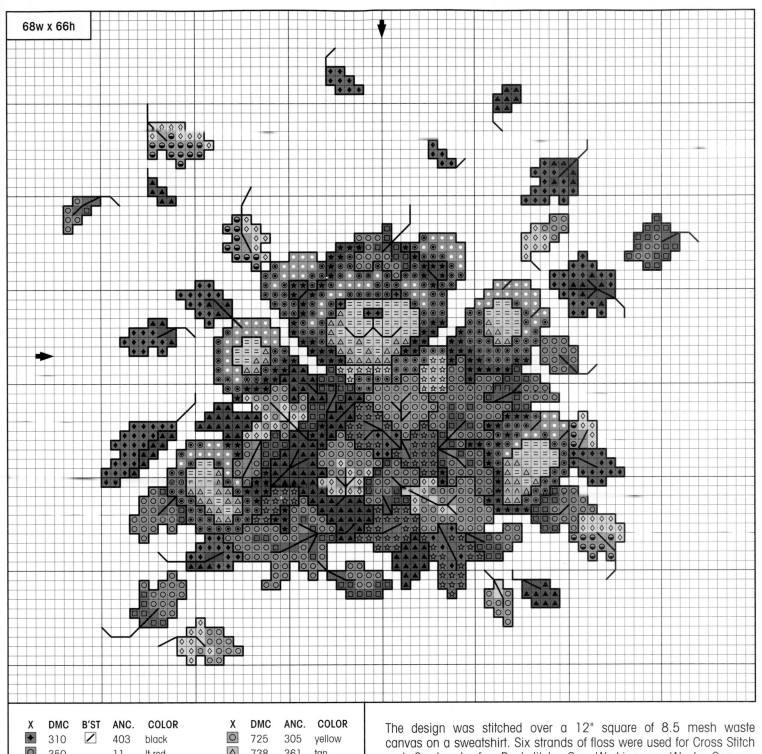

68w x 66h

X	DMC	B'ST	ANC.	COLOR	X	DMC	ANC.	COLOR
★	310	✓	403	black	◐	725	305	yellow
◎	350		11	lt red	△	738	361	tan
★	435		1046	dk brown	=	739	387	lt tan
◉	436		1045	brown	⊖	782	308	gold
⊙	437		362	lt brown	◇	783	307	lt gold
▲	720		326	dk orange	☆	813	161	lt blue
◆	721		324	orange	▣	817	13	red
✦	722		323	lt orange	◉	826	161	blue

The design was stitched over a 12" square of 8.5 mesh waste canvas on a sweatshirt. Six strands of floss were used for Cross Stitch and 2 strands for Backstitch. See Working on Waste Canvas, page 143.

Design by Ginny Fraser.
Needlework adaptation by Kathy Elrod.

107

Faced with an assortment of tempting goodies that are too delicious to resist, this teddy issues a chocolate-lover's plea. The winsome design is stitched on an apron to please a cook.

Deliver me from evil but leave my chocolate alone!

X	DMC	¼X	B'ST	ANC.	COLOR
•	blanc			2	white
▬	318			399	dk grey
■	321	◢	◿	9046	red
Σ	335			38	dk pink
8	415			398	grey
◆	433	◢		358	lt brown
▲	434			310	vy lt brown
▣	435			1046	vy dk tan
✚	436	◢		1045	dk tan
S	437	◢		362	tan
◉	666	◢		46	lt red
2	738			361	lt tan
✳	739			387	vy lt tan
○	762			234	lt grey
V	801		◿	359	brown
★	839			360	dk beige brown
△	840			379	beige brown
❖	841			378	lt beige brown
☆	899			52	pink
◨	938			381	dk brown
◇	3326			36	lt pink
◙	3371	◢	◿	382	vy dk brown

The design was stitched over a 16" x 12" piece of 8.5 mesh waste canvas on the bib of an apron. Six strands of floss were used for Cross Stitch, 3 strands for red Backstitch and brown Backstitch, and 2 strands for all other Backstitch.

Working on Waste Canvas: Waste canvas is a special canvas that provides an evenweave grid for placing stitches on fabric. After the design is worked over the canvas, the canvas threads are removed, leaving the design on the fabric. The canvas is available in several mesh sizes.

Step 1. Cover edges of canvas with masking tape.

Step 2. Find desired placement for design; mark center of design on apron with a pin.

Step 3. Match center of canvas to pin. Use the blue threads in canvas to place canvas straight on apron; pin canvas to apron. Baste canvas to apron.

Step 4. Place apron in a screw-type hoop. We recommend a hoop that is large enough to encircle entire design.

Step 5. Using a sharp needle, work design, stitching from large holes to large holes.

Step 6. Trim canvas to within ¾" of design. Dampen canvas until it becomes limp. Using tweezers, pull out canvas threads one at a time.

Design by Debra Jordan Meyer.

105w x 68h

Embellishing a T-shirt, this "beary" cute ladybug is bound to bring lots of luck. A familiar children's rhyme enhances the summery design.

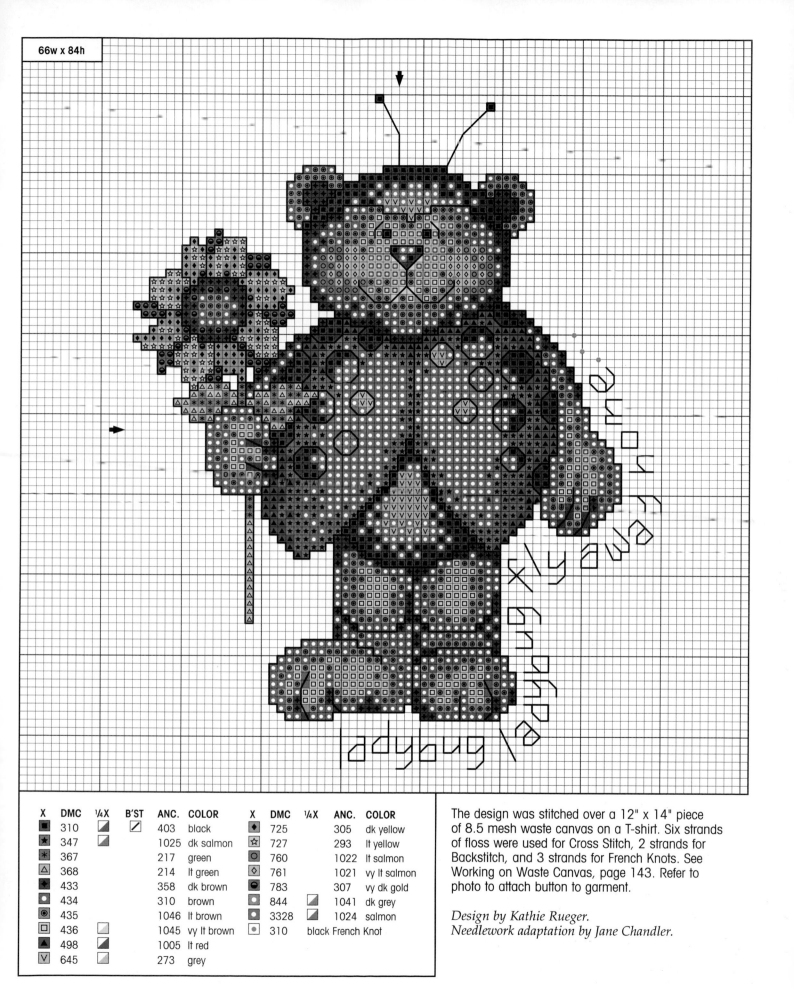

66w x 84h

X	DMC	¼X	B'ST	ANC.	COLOR
■	310	◨	◨	403	black
★	347	◨		1025	dk salmon
✳	367			217	green
△	368			214	lt green
◆	433			358	dk brown
◖	434			310	brown
◉	435			1046	lt brown
□	436	◨		1045	vy lt brown
▲	498	◨		1005	lt red
ⱽ	645	◨		273	grey

X	DMC	¼X	ANC.	COLOR
◆	725		305	dk yellow
☆	727		293	lt yellow
◐	760		1022	lt salmon
◇	761		1021	vy lt salmon
◒	783		307	vy dk gold
◖	844	◨	1041	dk grey
◖	3328	◨	1024	salmon
●	310			black French Knot

The design was stitched over a 12" x 14" piece of 8.5 mesh waste canvas on a T-shirt. Six strands of floss were used for Cross Stitch, 2 strands for Backstitch, and 3 strands for French Knots. See Working on Waste Canvas, page 143. Refer to photo to attach button to garment.

Design by Kathie Rueger.
Needlework adaptation by Jane Chandler.

111

Like flowers in a bouquet, when loved ones are gathered together they create something beautiful. This little country teddy bear and her feathered friends pass on this lesson of the heart.

59w x 79h

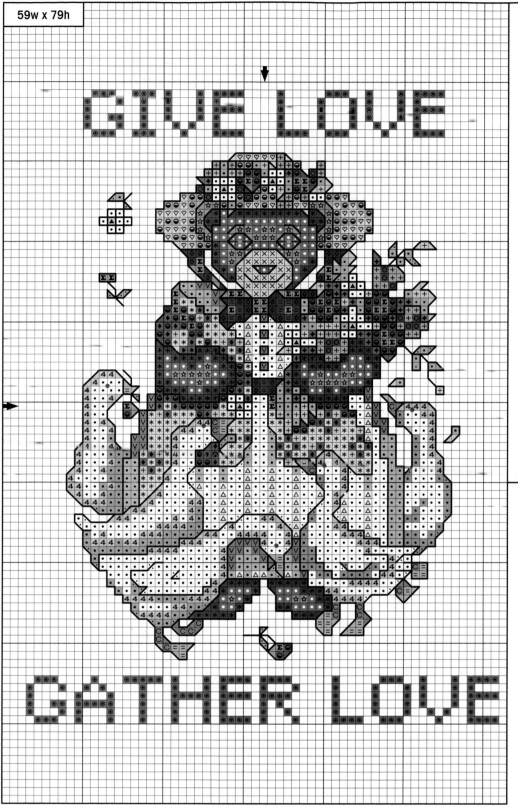

X	DMC	1/4X	B'ST	ANC.	COLOR
•	blanc	◢		2	white
◉	208	◢		110	purple
+	209	◢		109	lt purple
◈	309	◢		42	dk rose
▤	335			38	vy dk pink
✳	435	◢		1046	dk brown
▥	400	◢		1045	brown
☆	437	◢		362	lt brown
•	644	◢		830	beige
◖	676	◢		891	tan
♡	677	◢		886	lt tan
✕	738	◢		361	vy lt brown
▲	744			301	yellow
V	813	◢		161	blue
4	822	◢		390	lt beige
◉	825			162	dk blue
•	827	◢		160	lt blue
△	828	◿		9159	vy lt blue
✦	910	◢		229	dk green
•	912	◢		209	green
+	954	◢		203	lt green
◆	961			76	dk pink
Σ	962	◢		75	pink
✳	963	◢		73	vy lt pink
C	3340	◢		329	orange
☰	3341	◢		328	lt orange
◪	3371	◢	◤	382	brown black
◙	3716	◢		25	lt pink
◉	blanc				white French Knot
●	3371				brown black French Knot

The design was stitched over an 11" x 14" piece of 8.5 mesh waste canvas on a sweatshirt. Six strands of floss were used for Cross Stitch, 2 strands for Backstitch, and 4 strands for French Knots. See Working on Waste Canvas, page 143.

Design by Kim Stenbo for Figi Graphics. Needlework adaptation by Mike Vickery.

Any nurse will love this sweatshirt! Nurse Bear ministers to a tearful little patient in our tongue-in-cheek design.

X	DMC	¼X	B'ST	ANC.	COLOR
•	blanc			2	white
■	304			1006	dk red
■	310	◪	◪	403	black
★	318			399	dk grey
S	321		◪	9046	red
=	415	◪		398	grey
◉	433	◪		358	vy dk brown
C	434	◪		310	dk brown
✕	435	◪		1046	brown
+	436	◪		1045	lt brown
○	738	◪		361	vy lt brown
•	310	black French Knot			
⊘	827	blue Lazy Daisy Stitch			

67w x 48h

The design was stitched over a 12" x 10" piece of 8.5 mesh waste canvas on a sweatshirt. Six strands of floss were used for Cross Stitch and 2 strands for Backstitch, French Knots, and Lazy Daisy Stitches. See Working on Waste Canvas, page 143.

Design by Kathie Rueger.

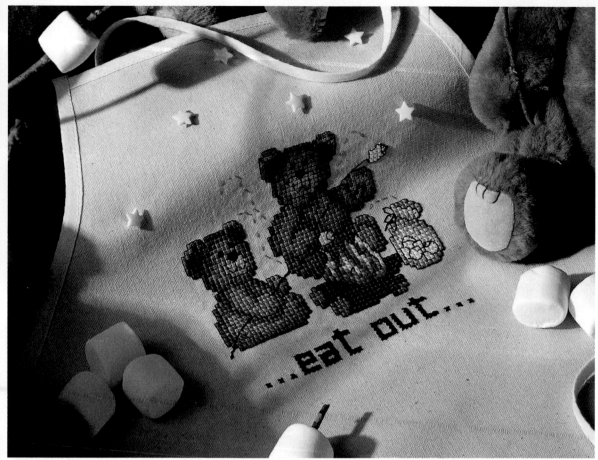

Who can resist the fun of "eating out" in the great outdoors? Certainly not these bears! Stitched on a canvas apron, our campfire design is just the thing for a summertime cookout.

56w x 51h

X	DMC	¼X	B'ST	ANC.	COLOR
•	blanc			2	white
O	307			289	yellow
8	310		∕	403	black
C	318			399	grey
	414		∕	235	dk grey
◎	415			398	lt grey
▪	434			310	vy dk tan
X	435			1046	dk tan
S	436			1045	tan
❖	437			362	lt tan
+	738			361	vy lt tan
▢	740		∕	316	orange
Σ	762			234	vy lt grey
≡	801			359	brown
▣	898		∕	360	dk brown
V	946			332	dk orange
●	310		black French Knot		

The design was stitched over an 11" x 10" piece of 8.5 mesh waste canvas on the bib of an apron. Six strands of floss were used for Cross Stitch, 4 strands for dk brown Backstitch, and 2 strands for all other Backstitch and French Knots. See Working on Waste Canvas, page 143. Refer to photo for placement of star buttons.

Design by Kathie Rueger.

For The Fun Of It

Laughter is good for the soul, as the teddy bears in this collection all know! Portraying events from everyday life, these fun-filled designs invite you to smile, be happy, and make gloomy days sunny. Anyone who's ever faced a mountain of laundry will appreciate Another Day in Paradise, *which makes light of housework. You'll find other humorous observations about life as you turn the pages, along with poignant images of memorable moments such as a child's first haircut.*

62w x 77h

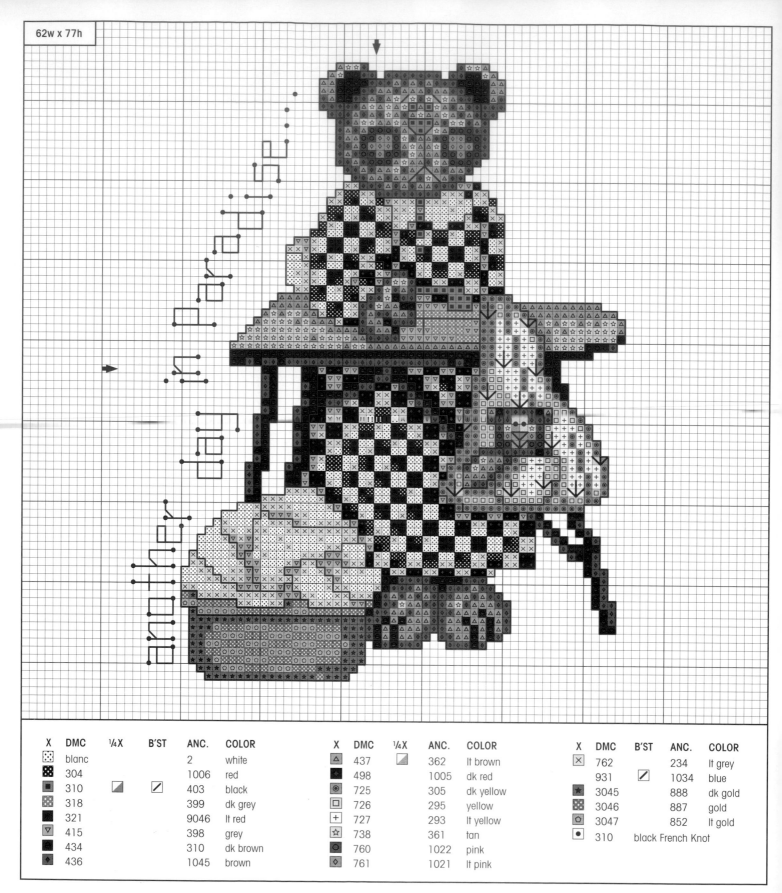

X	DMC	¼X	B'ST	ANC.	COLOR	X	DMC	¼X	ANC.	COLOR	X	DMC	B'ST	ANC.	COLOR
	blanc			2	white	△	437	◩	362	lt brown	☒	762		234	lt grey
☒	304			1006	red	✦	498		1005	dk red		931	◩	1034	blue
■	310	◩	◩	403	black	◉	725		305	dk yellow	★	3045		888	dk gold
▦	318			399	dk grey	□	726		295	yellow	☒	3046		887	gold
■	321			9046	lt red	+	727		293	lt yellow	◎	3047		852	lt gold
▽	415			398	grey	☆	738		361	tan	•	310			black French Knot
■	434			310	dk brown	◎	760		1022	pink					
◆	436			1045	brown	◇	761		1021	lt pink					

The design was stitched on a 13" x 14" piece of Ivory Aida (14 ct). Three strands of floss were used for Cross Stitch and 1 strand for Backstitch and French Knots. It was custom framed.

Design by Kathie Rueger. Needlework adaptation by Cara Gist.

Any time you're feeling "frazzled," our sweet teddy bear mug will make you smile. The cheery project will also make a fun gift for a busy friend

X	DMC	B'ST	ANC.	COLOR	X	DMC	ANC.	COLOR
ⅠⅠ	310	╱	403	black	═	738	361	tan
▼	433		358	dk brown	☆	739	387	lt tan
◆	435		1046	brown	✚	930	1035	dk blue
✕	436		1045	lt brown	✦	932	1033	blue
O	676		891	gold	◉	938	381	vy dk brown
>	677		886	lt gold	✿	3829		vy dk gold
▼	729		890	dk gold	•	310		black French Knot

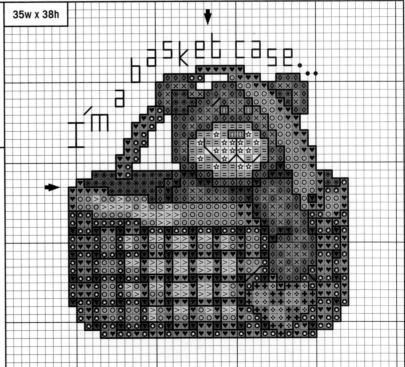

The design was stitched on a 10¼" x 3½" piece of Vinyl-Weave™ (14 ct). Three strands of floss were used for Cross Stitch and 1 strand for Backstitch and French Knots. It was inserted in a beige mug.

For design placement, fold vinyl in half, matching short edges. Center design on right half of vinyl if mug is to be used by a right-handed person or on the left half if mug is to be used by a left-handed person. Hand wash mug to protect stitchery.

Design by Kathie Rueger.
Needlework adaptation by Jane Chandler.

A nice long bubble bath is a luxurious way to escape the frustrations of the day! This nostalgic bear will help you get the message across when you need a little quiet time.

X	DMC	1/4X	B'ST	ANC.	COLOR	X	DMC	1/4X	B'ST	ANC.	COLOR	X	DMC	1/4X	B'ST	ANC.	COLOR
·	blanc			2	white	⊠	436			1045	vy lt brown	≡	963			73	vy lt pink
✳	310			403	black	V	437			362	tan	✶	3325			129	blue
·	318			399	grey		561			212	vy dk green	·	3716			25	lt pink
	322			978	vy dk blue	◉	632			936	rust brown	·	3747			120	vy lt purple
·	334			977	dk blue	Π	738			361	lt tan	H	3756			1037	vy lt blue
	335			38	dk rose	△	762			234	vy lt grey	2	3772			1007	vy dk pink
8	341			117	lt purple	★	775			128	lt blue	C	3773			1008	peach
☆	407			914	dk peach		794			175	purple blue	·	3811				lt aqua
	414			235	dk grey		801			359	dk brown	▲	3815				dk green
⊖	415			398	lt grey	○	950			4146	lt peach	◎	3816				green
▢	433			358	brown	+	961			76	dk pink	✤	3817				lt green
S	434			310	lt brown	◇	962			75	pink						

The design was stitched on a 10" square of Ivory Aida (18 ct). Two strands of floss were used for Cross Stitch and 1 strand for Backstitch. It was inserted in a purchased towel bar frame (6¼" dia. opening).

Design by Debra Jordan Bryan. Needlework adaptation by Jane Chandler.

This adorably grumpy teddy commemorates one of life's little milestones — a child's first haircut. The design can be custom framed for a sweet addition to a child's room or a friend's bear collection, or you can personalize it for an unforgettable keepsake.

Fast and efficient, the microwave oven gives busy cooks more leisure time to enjoy family, friends, and of course, cross stitching!

MICROWAVE

SUPER CHEF

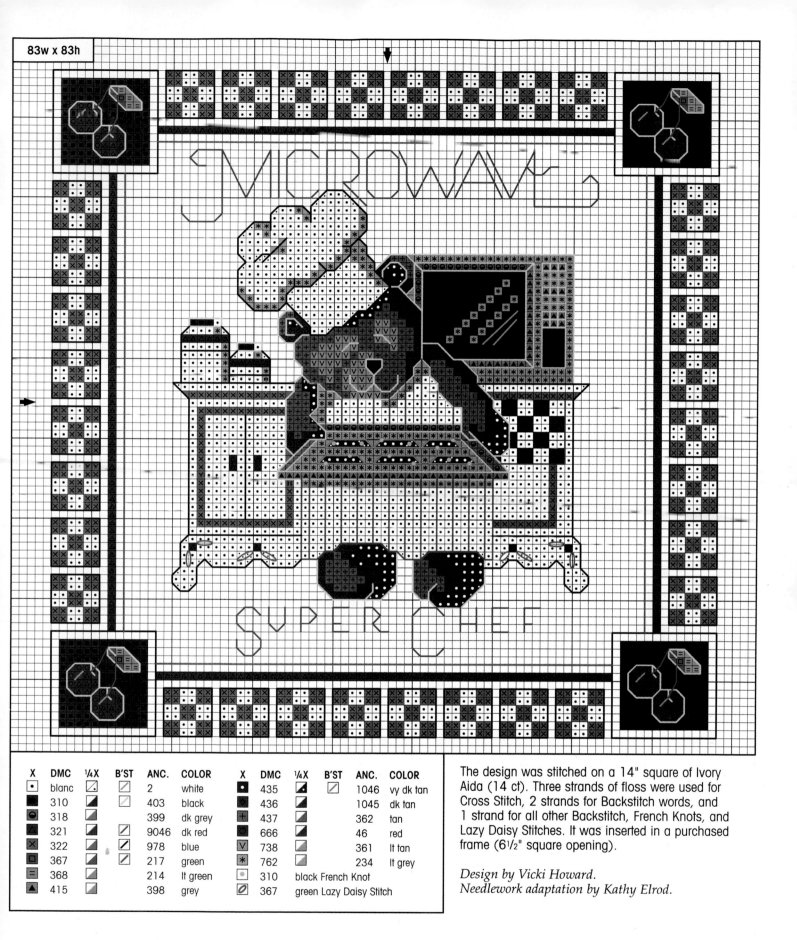

83w x 83h

X	DMC	¼X	B'ST	ANC.	COLOR	X	DMC	¼X	B'ST	ANC.	COLOR
•	blanc			2	white		435			1046	vy dk tan
■	310			403	black	◆	436			1045	dk tan
◐	318			399	dk grey	+	437			362	tan
▲	321			9046	dk red	◨	666			46	red
✕	322			978	blue	V	738			361	lt tan
▣	367			217	green	*	762			234	lt grey
≡	368			214	lt green	•	310			black French Knot
▲	415			398	grey	⬭	367			green Lazy Daisy Stitch

The design was stitched on a 14" square of Ivory Aida (14 ct). Three strands of floss were used for Cross Stitch, 2 strands for Backstitch words, and 1 strand for all other Backstitch, French Knots, and Lazy Daisy Stitches. It was inserted in a purchased frame (6½" square opening).

Design by Vicki Howard.
Needlework adaptation by Kathy Elrod.

Grandma's fresh, home-baked cookies are every child's dream! This pot holder and mug are just the thing for snack time.

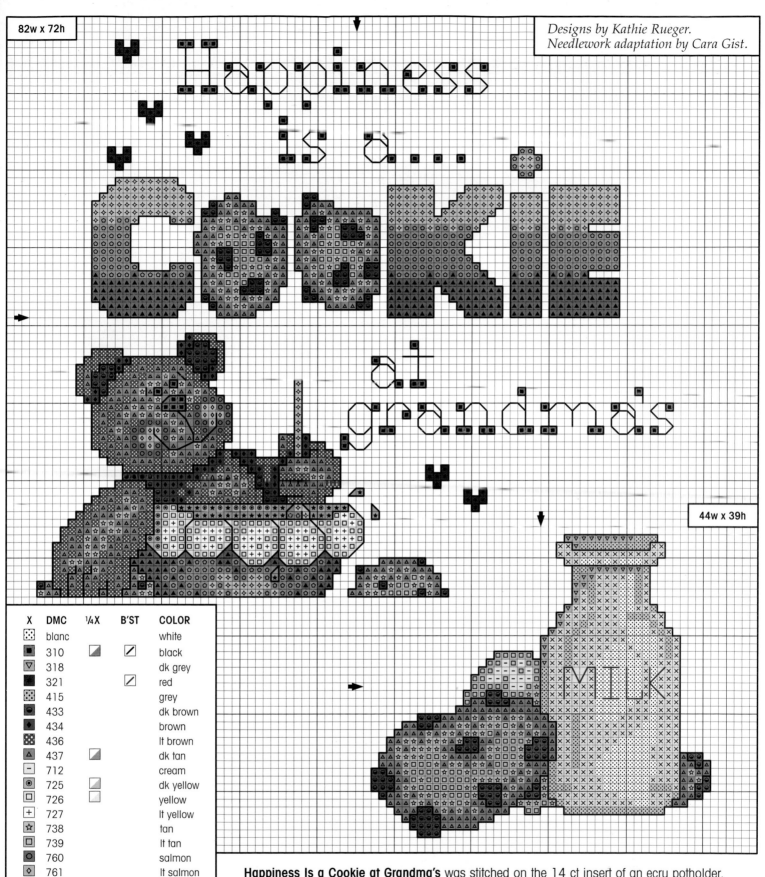

82w x 72h

Designs by Kathie Rueger.
Needlework adaptation by Cara Gist.

44w x 39h

X	DMC	¼X	B'ST	COLOR
▦	blanc			white
■	310	◪	◪	black
▽	318			dk grey
◼	321		◪	red
▨	415			grey
◉	433			dk brown
◆	434			brown
▩	436			lt brown
△	437	◪		dk tan
−	712			cream
◉	725	◪		dk yellow
□	726	◪		yellow
+	727			lt yellow
✫	738			tan
◻	739			lt tan
◯	760			salmon
◇	761			lt salmon
✕	762			lt grey
★	783	◪		gold
▲	930	◪		dk blue
⬠	931	◪		blue
✦	932	◪		lt blue
•	310			black French Knot

Happiness Is a Cookie at Grandma's was stitched on the 14 ct insert of an ecru potholder. Three strands of floss were used for Cross Stitch and 1 strand for Backstitch and French Knots.

Cookies and Milk was stitched on a 10¼" x 3½" piece of Vinyl-Weave™ (14 ct). Three strands of floss were used for Cross Stitch and 1 strand for Backstitch. It was inserted in a white mug.

For design placement, fold vinyl in half, matching short edges. Center design on right half of vinyl if mug is to be used by a right-handed person or on the left half if mug is to be used by a left-handed person. Hand wash mug to protect stitchery.

129

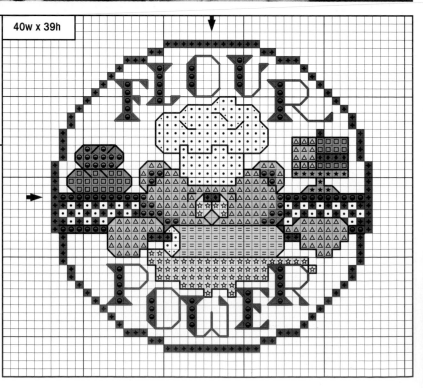

40w x 39h

X	DMC	¼X	B'ST	COLOR	X	DMC	¼X	B'ST	COLOR
•	blanc			white	★	666			red
	310		✓	black	☆	739			lt tan
◐	434			dk tan	◧	798		✓	blue
△	437			tan	=	809			lt blue
★	563			green	◆	898			brown
▣	632			mocha					

The design was stitched on a 7" square of White Aida (14 ct). Three strands of floss were used for Cross Stitch and 1 strand for Backstitch and French Knots. It was stiffened and made into a gift tag.

For stiffened tag, cut one piece of medium-weight cream fabric same size as stitched piece for backing. Apply a heavy coat of fabric stiffener to back of stitched piece using a small foam brush. Matching wrong sides, place stitched piece on backing fabric, smoothing stitched piece while pressing fabric pieces together; allow to dry. Apply fabric stiffener to backing fabric and allow to dry. Refer to photo to trim stitched piece. Using a hole punch, cut a hole at top of tag.

Design by Linda Gillum.

A bucketful of bubbles makes bathtime more bearable for this endearing teddy. The lighthearted piece is ideal for the bathroom!

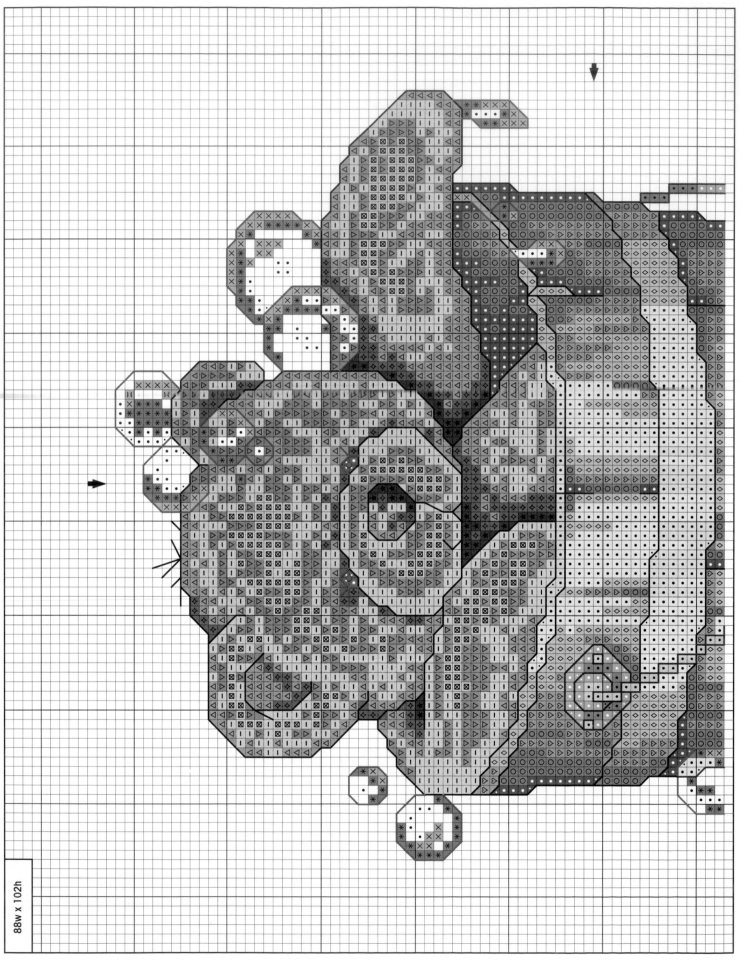

88w x 102h

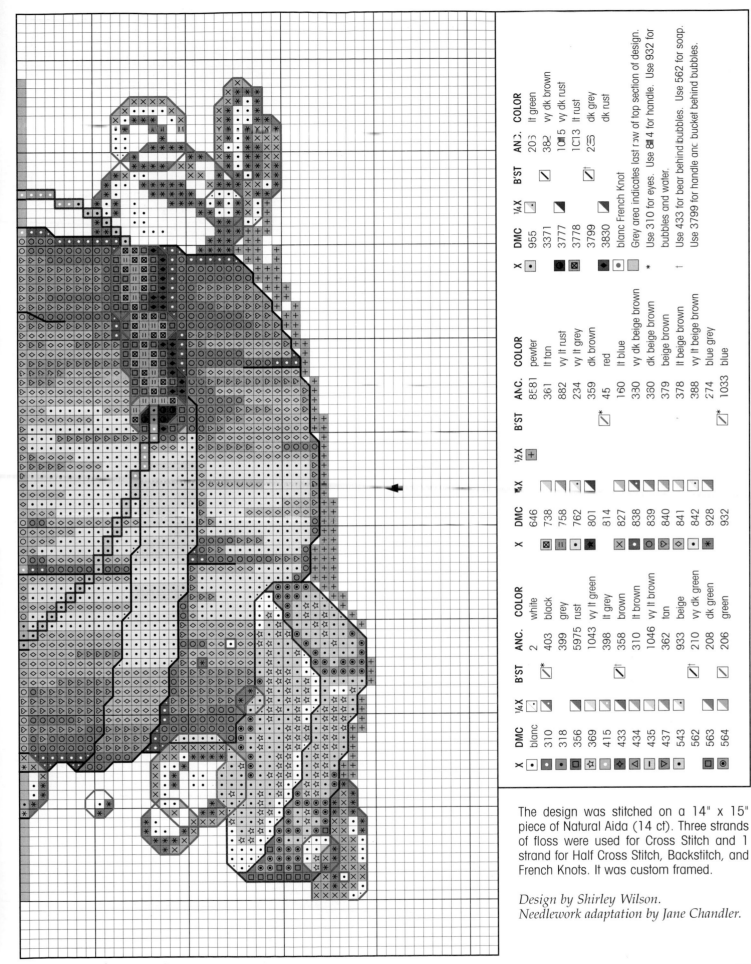

X	DMC	ANC.	COLOR
	955	203	lt green
	3371	382	vy dk brown
	3777	1015	vy dk rust
	3778	1013	lt rust
	3799	236	dk grey
	3830		dk rust
	blanc French Knot		

Grey area indicates last row of top section of design. Use 310 for eyes. Use 814 for handle. Use 932 for bubbles and water. Use 433 for bear behind bubbles. Use 562 for soap. Use 3799 for handle and bucket behind bubbles.

X	DMC	ANC.	COLOR
	646	8581	pewter
	738	361	lt tan
	758	882	vy lt rust
	762	234	vy lt grey
	801	359	dk brown
	814	45	red
	827	160	lt blue
	838	330	vy dk beige brown
	839	360	dk beige brown
	840	379	beige brown
	841	378	lt beige brown
	842	388	vy lt beige brown
	928	274	blue grey
	932	1033	blue

X	DMC	ANC.	COLOR
	blanc	2	white
	310	403	black
	318	399	grey
	356	5975	rust
	369	1043	vy lt green
	415	398	lt grey
	433	358	brown
	434	310	lt brown
	435	1046	vy lt brown
	437	362	tan
	543	933	beige
	562	210	vy dk green
	563	208	dk green
	564	206	green

The design was stitched on a 14" x 15" piece of Natural Aida (14 ct). Three strands of floss were used for Cross Stitch and 1 strand for Half Cross Stitch, Backstitch, and French Knots. It was custom framed.

Design by Shirley Wilson.
Needlework adaptation by Jane Chandler.

Cuddlers young and old will find comfort in this cozy afghan — just like these two little cubs snuggled against their mama's soft shoulders. The touching trio will steal your heart away.

73w x 76h

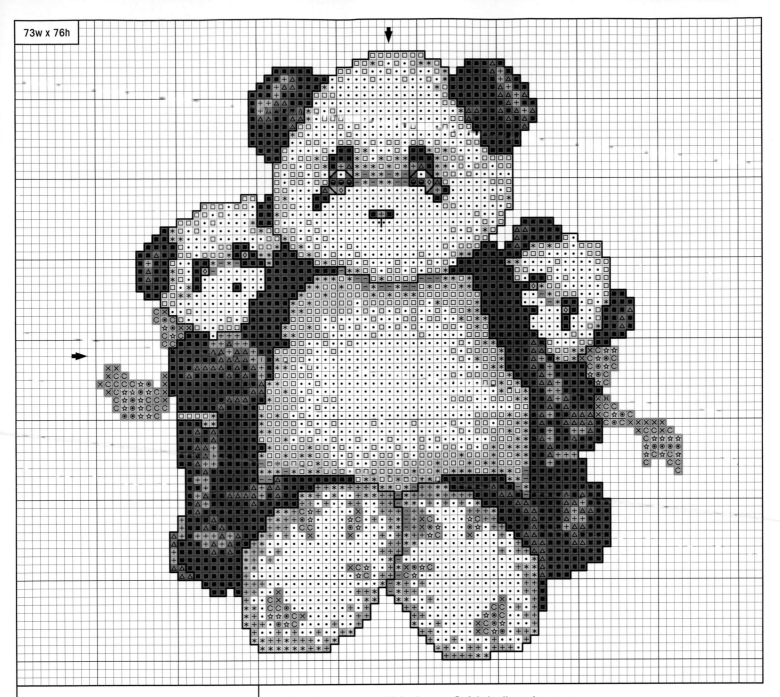

X	DMC	¼X	B'ST	ANC.	COLOR
•	blanc			2	white
■	310	◩	◿	403	black
+	317	◩		400	lt grey
	347		◿	1025	vy dk pink
◇	434	◩		310	lt brown
–	642			392	dk tan
*	644			830	tan
C	760			1022	pink
☆	761			1021	lt pink
◕	801	◩		359	brown
▢	822			390	lt tan
X	3712			1023	dk pink
◉	3713			1020	vy lt pink
△	3799	◩		236	grey

The design was stitched over 2 fabric threads on a 45" x 58" piece (standard afghan size) of Antique Blue Anne Cloth (18 ct). Six strands of floss were used for Cross Stitch and 2 strands for Backstitch. Refer to Diagram for placement of design on fabric. It was made into an afghan.

For afghan, cut selvages from fabric; measure 5½" from raw edge of fabric and pull out one fabric thread. Fringe fabric up to missing thread. Repeat for each side. Tie an overhand knot at each corner with 4 horizontal and 4 vertical fabric threads. Working from corners, use 8 fabric threads for each knot until all threads are knotted. Refer to photo to add buttons and ribbon as desired.

Design from Heartprint Greeting Cards, Inc.
Original artwork by Jan Jameson.
Needlework adaptation by Mike Vickery.

DIAGRAM

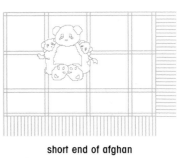

short end of afghan

135

Sweet treats can be "unbearably" tempting! While luring us into the kitchen to bake scrumptious goodies, this delightful design reminds us not to eat too many of them.

LIFE IS FULL OF

UPS AND POUNDS!

LIFE IS FULL OF

UPS AND POUNDS!

84w x 98h

X	DMC	¼X	B'ST	ANC.	COLOR	X	DMC	¼X	B'ST	ANC.	COLOR
•	blanc			2	white	☆	680			901	dk yellow
◉	309			42	pink	2	738			361	vy lt tan
+	433			358	brown		798			131	vy dk blue
❖	434			310	lt brown	✕	799			136	dk blue
‖	435			1046	dk tan	□	800			144	lt blue
△	436			1045	tan	◒	809			130	blue
=	437			362	lt tan	✳	816			1005	dk pink
S	562			210	green	▲	898			360	dk brown
V	563			208	lt green	◇	3326			36	lt pink
O	676			891	yellow	●	898				dk brown French Knot

The design was stitched on a 14" x 15" piece of Beige Aida (14 ct). Two strands of floss were used for Cross Stitch and 1 strand for Backstitch and French Knots. It was inserted in a cookbook holder (7" x 8" opening).

Design by Deb Meyer for Figi Graphics.

137

Spell out your love for Teddy with this colorful alphabet! We used the letters to personalize a shirt, but you can use your imagination to create a variety of projects.

X	DMC	¼X	B'ST	ANC.	COLOR
■	208	◩		110	purple
	310	◩	◪	403	black
▲	434	◩		310	brown
−	437	◩		362	lt brown
▣	444	◩		290	yellow
✦	602	◩		63	pink
✚	700	◩		228	green
✚	740	◩		316	orange
▲	825	◩		162	blue
●	310				black French Knot

The name "JOSH" was stitched over a 10" x 5" piece of 8.5 mesh waste canvas on a sweatshirt. Six strands of floss were used for Cross Stitch, 2 strands for Backstitch, and 4 strands for French Knots. See Working on Waste Canvas, page 143.

Design by
Terrie Lee Steinmeyer© 1995

With just a few loving stitches, a timeworn friend like Teddy can feel like new! This whimsical wall hanging is great for the sewing room.

...teddy bear repair...

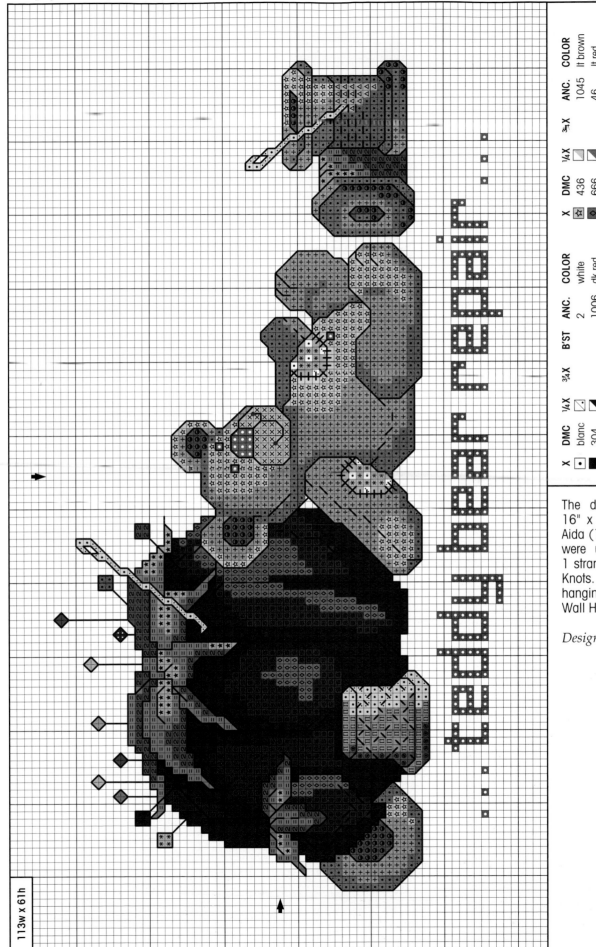

The design was stitched on a 16" x 12" piece of Antique White Aida (14 ct). Three strands of floss were used for Cross Stitch and 1 strand for Backstitch and French Knots. It was made into a wall hanging. See "Teddy Bear Repair" Wall Hanging Finishing, page 144.

Design by Kathie Rueger.

113w x 61h

141

GENERAL INSTRUCTIONS

WORKING WITH CHARTS

How to Read Charts: Each of the designs is shown in chart form. Each colored square on the chart represents one Cross Stitch or one Half Cross Stitch. Each colored triangle on the chart represents one One-Quarter Stitch or one Three-Quarter Stitch. Black or colored dots represent French Knots. Black or colored ovals represent Lazy Daisy Stitches. The straight lines on the chart indicate Backstitch. When a French Knot, Lazy Daisy Stitch, or Backstitch covers a square, the symbol is omitted or a reduced symbol is shown.

Each chart is accompanied by a color key. This key indicates the color of floss to use for each stitch on the chart. The headings on the color key are for Cross Stitch (**X**), DMC color number (**DMC**), One-Quarter Stitch (**¼X**), Three-Quarter Stitch (**¾X**), Half Cross Stitch (**½X**), Backstitch (**B'ST**), Anchor color number (**ANC**), and color name (**COLOR**). Color key columns should be read vertically and horizontally to determine type of stitch and floss color.

How to Determine Finished Size: The finished size of your design will depend on the thread count per inch of the fabric being used. To determine the finished size of the design on different fabrics, divide the number of squares (stitches) in the width of the charted design by the thread count of the fabric. For example, a charted design with a width of 80 squares worked on 14 count Aida will yield a design 5¾" wide. Repeat for the number of squares (stitches) in the height of the charted design. (**Note:** To work over two fabric threads, divide the number of squares by one-half the thread count.) Then add the amount of background you want plus a generous amount for finishing.

Where to Start: The horizontal and vertical centers of the charted design are shown by arrows. You may start at any point on the charted design, but be sure the design will be centered on the fabric. Locate the center of fabric by folding in half, top to bottom and again left to right. On the charted design, count the number of squares from the center of the chart to the determined starting point; then from the fabric's center, count out the same number of fabric threads.

STITCH DIAGRAMS

Counted Cross Stitch (X): For horizontal rows, work stitches in two journeys (**Fig. 1**). For vertical rows, complete each stitch as shown (**Fig. 2**). When working over two fabric threads, work Cross Stitch as shown in **Fig. 3**. When the chart shows a Backstitch crossing a colored square (**Fig. 4**), a Cross Stitch should be worked first; then the Backstitch (**Fig. 9 or 10**) should be worked on top of the Cross Stitch.

Fig. 1

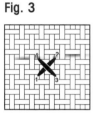

Fig. 2

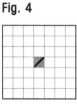

Fig. 3

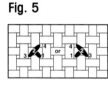

Fig. 4

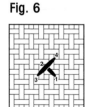

Quarter Stitch (¼X and ¾X): Come up at 1 (**Fig. 5**); then split fabric thread to go down at 2. When stitches 1-4 are worked in the same color, the resulting stitch is called a Three-Quarter Stitch (**¾X**). When working over 2 fabric threads, work Quarter Stitches as shown in **Fig. 6**.

Fig. 5

Fig. 6

Half Cross Stitch (½X): This stitch is one journey of the Cross Stitch and is worked from lower left to upper right as shown in **Fig. 7**. When working over two fabric threads, work Half Cross Stitch as shown in **Fig. 8**.

Fig. 7

Fig. 8

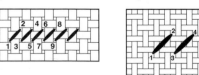

Backstitch (B'ST): For outline detail, Backstitch should be worked after the design has been completed (**Fig. 9**). When working over two fabric threads, work Backstitch as shown in **Fig. 10**.

Fig. 9

Fig. 10

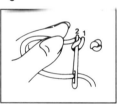

French Knot: Bring needle up at 1. Wrap floss once around needle and insert needle at 2, holding floss with non-stitching fingers (**Fig. 11**). Tighten knot; then pull needle through fabric, holding floss until it must be released. For larger knot, use more strands; wrap only once.

Fig. 11

Lazy Daisy Stitch: Bring needle up at 1 and make a loop. Go down at 1 and come up at 2, keeping floss below point of needle (**Fig. 12**). Pull needle through and go down at 2 to anchor loop, completing stitch. (**Note:** To support stitches, it may be helpful to go down in edge of next fabric thread when anchoring loop.)

Fig. 12

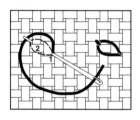

142

STITCHING TIPS

Working over Two Fabric Threads: Use the sewing method instead of the stab method when working over two fabric threads. To use the sewing method, keep your stitching hand on the right side of the fabric (instead of stabbing the fabric with the needle and taking your stitching hand to the back of the fabric to pick up the needle). With the sewing method, you take the needle down and up with one stroke instead of two. To add support to stitches, it is important that the first Cross Stitch is placed on the fabric with stitch 1-2 beginning and ending where a vertical fabric thread crosses over a horizontal fabric thread (**Fig. 13**). When the first stitch is in the correct position, the entire design will be placed properly, with vertical fabric threads supporting each stitch.

Fig. 13

Working on Waste Canvas: Waste canvas (also known as tear-away cloth or waste cloth) is a special canvas that provides an evenweave grid for placing stitches on fabric. After the design is worked over the canvas, the canvas threads are removed, leaving the design on the fabric. Most canvas has blue parallel threads every fifth square to aid in counting and in placing the canvas straight on the fabric. The blue threads may be placed horizontally or vertically. The canvas is available in several mesh sizes. Use lightweight, nonfusible interfacing on wrong side of fabric to give a firmer stitching base. We recommend a screw-type hoop that is large enough to encircle the entire design. Use a #24 tapestry needle for knit fabric. Use a sharp embroidery needle for tightly knit or tightly woven fabric. To ensure smoother stitches, separate floss strands and realign them before threading the needle.

Step 1. Cut waste canvas 2" larger than design size on all sides. Cut interfacing same size as canvas. To prevent raw edges of canvas from marring fabric, cover edges of canvas with masking tape.

Step 2. Find desired placement for design; mark center of design on garment with a pin.

Step 3. Match center of canvas to pin. Use the blue threads in canvas to place canvas

straight on garment; pin canvas to garment. Pin interfacing to wrong side of garment. To prevent canvas from slipping, especially on large designs, baste securely around edge of canvas through all three thicknesses. Then baste from corner to corner and from side to side as shown in **Fig. 14**.

Fig. 14

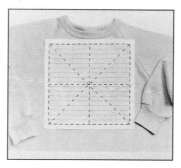

Step 4. Place garment in hoop. The hoop helps keep the area not being stitched out of the way. Roll excess fabric, including back of garment, over top edge of hoop and pin in place (**Fig. 15**).

Fig. 15

Step 5. Work design following Stitch Diagrams.

Step 6. Trim canvas to within ³/₄" of design. Use a sponge or spray bottle of water to dampen canvas until it becomes limp. Using tweezers, pull out canvas threads one at a time (**Fig. 16**).

Fig. 16

Step 7. Trim interfacing close to design.

FINISHING TECHNIQUES
AFGHAN FINISHING

Cut selvages from fabric; measure 5¹/₂" from raw edge of fabric and pull out one fabric thread. Repeat for each side. Tie an overhand knot at each corner with 4 horizontal and 4 vertical fabric threads. Working from corners, use 8 fabric threads for each knot until all threads are knotted (**Fig. 17**). Refer to diagram below for placement of design on afghan.

Fig. 17

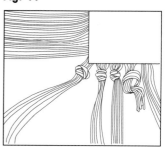

Diagram

BABY AFGHAN FINISHING

Cut selvage from fabric. Machine stitch along raised threads around outside edge of afghan. Fringe fabric to machine-stitched lines. Refer to diagram below for placement of design on afghan.

Diagram

MINI PILLOW FINISHING

With design centered on fabric, cut stitched piece and backing fabric (same fabric as stitched piece) desired width and height plus ¹/₂" on all four sides to allow for fringe. Matching wrong sides and raw edges, use desired floss color to cross stitch fabric pieces together ¹/₂" from bottom and side edges. Stuff pillow with polyester fiberfill; cross stitch across top of pillow ¹/₂" from edges. Fringe fabric to one square from cross-stitched lines. If desired, whipstitch ribbon to pillow for hanger.

143

WALL HANGING FINISHING

Continued from page 93.
For wall hanging, you will need 44/45"w cotton or cotton blend fabrics ($^5/_8$ yd of tan, $^1/_8$ yd of red, $^1/_2$ yd of black, $^1/_4$ yd of muslin, and $^5/_8$ yd of black for backing and hanging tabs); 8" x $25^1/_2$" piece of $^1/_2$" thick low-loft craft batting; straight pins; black fine-point fabric marker; thread; hand-sewing needle; black acrylic paint; foam brush; 19" length of $^7/_8$" dia. wooden dowel and end caps; and wood glue.

1. Center design and trim stitched piece to measure 10" x $11^1/_2$".

2. (**Note**: All fabric pieces must be cut straight and on grain in order for piecing to be accurate; therefore, it is important to take your time when measuring and cutting.) Referring to fabric table below, cut fabric pieces.

Wall Hanging Fabric Pieces			
Fabric Piece	Fabric	Quantity	Size
A	tan	2	10" x $3^1/_2$"
B	tan	2	$11^1/_2$" x $3^1/_2$"
C	red	4	$3^1/_2$" x $3^1/_2$"
D	black	2	$16^1/_2$" x $2^1/_2$"
E	black	3	18" x $2^1/_2$"
F	muslin	1	15" x $5^1/_2$"
G	tan	2	$2^1/_2$" x $5^1/_2$"
H	black	4	4" x $8^1/_2$"

Note: For **Steps 3-8**, match right sides, raw edges, and refer to Diagram to sew fabric pieces together using a $^1/_2$" seam allowance. Press seam allowance toward darker fabric whenever possible.

3. Sew one **A** fabric piece to top of stitched piece and one to bottom of stitched piece.

4. Sew one **C** fabric piece to each short end of each **B** fabric piece.

5. Sew a **B/C** fabric strip to each side of stitched piece.

6. Sew one **D** fabric piece to each side.

7. Sew one **E** fabric piece to top and one to bottom.

8. Sew one **G** fabric piece to each short end of **F** fabric piece. Sew remaining **E** fabric piece to top of **F/G**; sew **E/F/G** to top of **E**.

9. For hanging tab, fold one **H** fabric piece in half, matching right sides and long raw edges; using a $^1/_2$" seam allowance, sew long edges together. Turn tab right side out and press. Repeat for three remaining **H** fabric pieces.

10. Matching raw edges, fold each hanging tab in half and press. Referring to Diagram for spacing, match raw edges of each hanging tab with top raw edge of right side of wall hanging and pin in place. (Each outer tab should be placed $^1/_2$" from side edge to allow for sewing backing and front together.) Baste hanging tabs to wall hanging $^1/_4$" from raw edge.

11. Cut backing fabric same size as wall hanging front. For remainder of this step, match raw edges and smooth wrinkles from each layer. Place wall hanging front right side up on flat work surface. Place backing fabric wrong side up on top of wall hanging front. Place batting on top of backing fabric; pin layers together.

12. Using a $^1/_2$" seam allowance and leaving approx. 4" at center bottom of wall hanging open for turning, sew layers together. Trim corners diagonally. Turn right side out. Blindstitch opening closed.

13. Referring to photo, use a black fine-point fabric marker to write "Happy Thanksgiving" on **F**.

14. Paint wooden dowel and end caps using black acrylic paint and foam brush; allow to dry. Glue end caps to ends of wooden dowel. Insert wooden dowel through hanging tabs.

Diagram

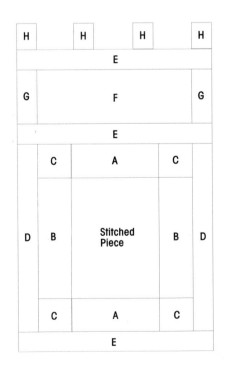

"TEDDY BEAR REPAIR" WALL HANGING FINISHING

Continued from page 141.
(**Note**: Use a $^1/_2$" seam allowance for all seams.)

1. For wall hanging front, center design and trim stitched piece to measure 11" x $7^1/_2$".

2. For inner border, cut two $7^1/_2$" x $2^1/_2$" strips of fabric. Matching right sides and raw edges, sew strips to sides of stitched piece. Press seam allowances toward strips. Cut two $2^1/_2$" x 14" strips of fabric. Matching right sides and raw edges, sew strips to top and bottom of stitched piece and attached strips. Press seam allowances toward strips.

3. For outer border, cut two $10^1/_2$" x 2" strips of fabric. Matching right sides and raw edges, sew strips to sides of stitched piece and attached strips. Press seam allowances toward strips. Cut two 2" x 16" strips of fabric. Matching right sides and raw edges, sew strips to top and bottom of stitched piece and attached strips. Press seam allowances toward strips to complete wall hanging front.

4. To make hanging loops, cut three 7" x 4" pieces of fabric. For each loop, match right sides and fold in half lengthwise; sew along raw edges opposite fold. Turn right side out and press. Matching raw edges, fold loop in half; press. Referring to photo for placement, match right sides and raw edges and baste loops to top of wall hanging front.

5. For backing, cut a piece of fabric same size as wall hanging front. Cut a piece of craft fleece same size as backing fabric. Matching right sides and raw edges, place backing fabric on wall hanging front; place craft fleece on backing fabric. Pin layers together.

6. Beginning at bottom edge and leaving an opening for turning, sew layers together. Trim craft fleece seam allowance close to stitching; trim corners diagonally. Turn right side out, carefully pushing corners outward. Whipstitch opening closed. Insert dowel through loops.